*Workers Write!*

**Tales from the Courtroom**

Edited by David LaBounty

Blue Cubicle Press

Published by
BLUE CUBICLE PRESS, LLC
Post Office Box 250382
Plano, Texas 75025-0382

© 2011 by Blue Cubicle Press, LLC. All rights reserved.
Printed in the United States of America.

ISSN 1556-715X
ISBN 978-0-9827136-2-4

First Printing
17 2011 500

No part of this book may be reproduced or transmitted in any form or by any means, electronic or mechanical, including photocopying and recording, or by any information storage and retrieval system without the prior written permission of the copyright owner unless such copying is expressly permitted by federal copyright law. Blue Cubicle Press is not authorized to grant permission for further uses of copyrighted selections reprinted in this book without the permission of their owners. Permission must be obtained from individual copyright owners as identified herein. Address requests for permission to make copies of Blue Cubicle Press material to Permissions, Blue Cubicle Press, P.O. Box 250382, Plano, TX 75025-0382.

This book contains works of fiction. Names, characters, incidents, and places are the products of the authors' imaginations or are used fictitiously. Any resemblance to actual events, locales, or persons, living or dead, is coincidental.

Forward by David LaBounty. Copyright © 2011 by Blue Cubicle Press, LLC.

Original cover artwork by Linda K. Smith. Copyright © 2011 by Linda K. Smith

Credits:

A version of *Affirmed* appeared in the December 2006 – February 2007 issue of *Skyline Literary Magazine*. That version was reprinted in the June 2007 issue of the *Journal of Consumer Attorneys Association for Southern California*.

"Pled" originally appeared in *Arizona Attorney Magazine*.

# CONTENTS

# FORWARD

Stop me if you've heard this one: Two lawyers and a court reporter walk into a bar . . . .

No, wait. How many lawyers does it take to screw in a light bulb?

Oh yeah, who could forget the classic: Why did God make snakes before lawyers?

And on and on and on . . . .

I would venture a guess that lawyers, judges, and other courtroom employees don't rank high on popularity lists. Often thought of as greedy ambulance chasers, egotistical shysters, or heartless bench jockeys, those who have chosen legal careers are the focus of ridicule and the butt of jokes.

And yet, as shown by our choices in what we watch and read, we are truly fascinated with the profession. From *Inherit the Wind* to *Legally Blonde*, from Mason to Matlock to McBeal, courtroom drama (and comedy) makes for great theater.

But it's not just fiction that interests us. Afternoon television is filled with small-claims court shows that delight viewers with justices ridiculing regular folks. Newscasts lead off with celebrity arrests, and newspapers are filled with local and national court cases. We may make fun of the legal system and its employees, but we can't get enough of it.

That may be one reason why this was one of the easiest *Workers Write!* issues to put together. We received hundreds of submissions, most from practicing attorneys and judges still on the bench.

I wasn't too surprised (think John Grisham and Wallace Stevens). In the real world, I often work with lawyers, editing contracts and other legal language. Aside from their insistence on capitalizing every other word and making up phrases (Force majeure? Habeas corpus? I'll take Bands from the Early '80s for two hundred, Alex...), most are decent writers. They have an excellent understanding of language, and they can create well-written stories and poems.

And that's no joke.

David

# Workers Write!

## Tales from the Courtroom

## Bench Book

Judge not so often.
For the best part of your days,
hold stillness. Listen.

—*Charles Reynard*

# MOTHER, WITH CHILD

TONY PRESS

Summer sunlight pierced the high windows, angling to catch the dust that floated in the air before coating the ancient hardwood tables. At the longer table, in front of the empty jury box, sat two attorneys, one for the county and one *from* the county but "for the child," and a third person, a social worker, the three quietly chatting. Sitting opposite them, at a smaller table, silent, were the client and her attorney. Just below and to the right of the judge's perch, behind a tiny table, was a barely visible stenographer, and, below and to the judge's left, wearing a pistol on his right hip and sunglasses over his eyes, his belly craving escape above his wide black belt, was the bailiff, his surname, Newman, prominent on his chest. The unquiet silence ended when Newman stood and all came to order and the judge materialized from a door the attorney hadn't even seen. All rose but the one in whose name they were gathered, who remained elsewhere, in the county's children's shelter, the client's fourteen-month-old daughter: *In the matter of Alondra Cruz.*

The client was nineteen. The attorney was barely twenty-five, but even dressed in a suit as mature as she could abide, still she could have passed for twenty. Across the room, each of the county attorneys clearly possessed at least two full decades of adulthood, and the social worker's face suggested similar experience. The judge was beyond age. The client's attorney had never done this before. In fact, she'd never spoken out loud in court without a supervising attorney sitting discreetly at her shoulder, while still a law student, and then, none of her cases had involved a mother desperate for her child.

The client worked in alfalfa fields and with the dairy cows on a farm outside Monroe. At first, her husband's mother watched the child while they both worked, but after the husband and mother-in-law never returned from a funeral in Texas, she'd arranged with neighbors to look after her. The housing was stacked one against another. Everyone knew everyone, and everything about everyone, whether they wanted to or not. Most recently, a large eleven-year-old girl had watched the child, but when the mother trudged home two Fridays ago, she found neither baby nor sitter. Four pounding hours later, a deputy sheriff drove up in a shiny green police cruiser. From his car window he explained in increasingly louder and slower English to the mother and to her closest neighbor, who understood more English, that her daughter had been picked up at two in the afternoon, playing alone in the field near the filling station that doubled as the bus stop. The sheriff had no information on the eleven-year-old.

That was ten days ago. Finally, they were inside the vast courtroom that was the showpiece of the historic town square. The skinny, trembling mother, in her best dress, the one she carried with her when they crossed in March, the dress not as white as it once was, with the faintest hint of blue flowers in a semi-circle at her throat; behind her, alone among the rows of polished benches, the neighbor—the one who spoke a little English, and who, if the court permitted, would be called by the mother's attorney to explain what had happened, as interpreters were provided only in criminal cases—in a dark blue skirt and light blue button-down shirt; and the mother's attorney, who at times clasped her own hands together to keep them from shaking.

It could take all morning; it could take twenty minutes. She didn't know. She had rehearsed what she would say to the judge. Indeed, for three days, she'd practiced what she would say to anyone who would listen, and she had also rehearsed, both versions, depending on the judge's ruling, of what she would say to her client, in her own limited Spanish, after the hearing. As far from fluent in Spanish as she was, she felt a similar and more worrying inadequacy in the language and practice of law. Her white Corvair, once a sassy '66, now almost a dozen years old and as exhausted as an inanimate object could possibly be, was parked outside in front of the coffee shop where she'd spent an eternity waiting for the courthouse doors to open. She had woken at five thirty; arrived outside the courthouse at six thirty; nursed coffee, eggs, and home fries until eight thirty; and was the first to enter when the courthouse was finally open to the world. Now she waited, drumming the fingers of her left hand on top of her leather briefcase, her graduation gift to herself from the Sacred Feather shop on Madison's State Street. Her right hand rested on her right knee. Her eyes looked only at her two pens aligned next to the yellow legal pads, one completely blank, the other full of the facts and the law, organized as well as she was capable, coded in red and blue ink.

It could take all morning' it could take twenty minutes. She didn't know. How could she know?

Six days earlier, on a sweltering June morning that terminated three years of mind-numbing and distasteful law school classes, she had raised that right hand to be sworn in by the Supreme Court of Wisconsin. By the words of a black-robed justice whose name she had missed, she was now deemed a member of the state bar, a real lawyer. This moment, sitting next to her first client, the silent Anielka Cruz Collazo, was why she endured the three years, why she worked as a waitress and barmaid, why she incurred unfathomable debt, why she jeopardized her own marriage to the point where it jettisoned itself with barely a whimper: to get her ticket to practice. She survived by reminding herself every single day that it was nothing more than a glorified trade school, offering her the only chance she had to get the tools she wanted. This was why. All those years of complaining about the system, the haves and the have-nots, all her dreams of changing the world, or, at a minimum, evening the playing field: This was why.

Exactly twenty-six minutes later, the mother threw her arms around her, sobbing and shuddering so much they both almost fell. Their tears merged. Ninety minutes after that, the now-smiling social worker returned with a timid, then ecstatic, little girl.

She never saw them again. But had she possessed a locket on a silver chain, and had she worn it close to her heart, you would find them. They are always there.

## Family Law

### I

There are as many lawyer jokes
as embroidered aprons
at a church bazaar, or Hershey bars
at an AA meeting, or crows
in my neighbor's yard.
People tell me these jokes.
I say:

*"Everyone hates a lawyer*
*until he needs one,"*

which produces the sort of
silence during which I fill out
a retainer contract.

### II

Clients see the group toy box
under my receptionist's desk,
her tender smile,
the framed photo of my daughter,
and they feel I understand.
I do understand, but phone
slips pile up so tall on my desk
that the paperweight mouse gives up,
and I have to peel out
in the daycare parking lot
to arrive at court on time.

III

To the ones who call daily
to recount visitation arguments,
(the fact that ears were pierced
and gerbils purchased
to win affections), I say:

*"It's twenty dollars
every time I pick this phone up."*

This puts perspective
on how the child's laundry was returned,
how much sugar was given
to a hypoglycemic seven-year-old,
and whether entertainment
was PG-13.

IV

Eventually, homemade fudge
in plastic wrap
no longer arrives at my office.
The children have already
seen all the toys,
the other lawyer has a better suit,
and his file is color-coded.
The statement from my office
goes over thirty days.

When the trial date arrives, both sides
have found other relationships.
They are tired of meeting at Burger King
as neutral territory
when children are exchanged.
The judge splits the baby,
which the next door neighbor
could have predicted.

V
At last, the client makes
his final fee payment.
He says, during this visit,

*"This is how you lawyers all get rich."*

I tell my favorite lawyer joke,
the one about the five hundred dead lawyers.

Then, I take out the office garbage,
tie my Volvo door shut with twine,
and peel out toward the
daycare parking lot.

—*Kristin Roedell*

# MATT THE CLOSER

JEFFREY A. DICKERSON

He rose to address the jury. The top button of his suit coat buttoned, the red and blue striped tie knotted in a crisp Windsor, his hair just so, he strode to the center of the courtroom.

Feet inches apart, beneath black Ferragamos, back erect, shoulders set, yet relaxed, he looked into the jury box.

"This case is about Jackie Ann Sader." Matt stepped toward the defense table, to his secret spot, and said, "But it is also about corporate greed, greed that overrode the safety of those like Jackie Ann. Daycon consciously made the decision to save money and avoid safety just to ensure a higher margin of profit on its material. For that, Jackie Ann sits before you, transformed from a beautiful young woman into a monster for the rest of her life."

Juror One shifted in his seat. Juror Seven folded her arms. The rest sat mesmerized. Juror Four remembered that every time Matt talked about corporate greed over safety, he stood in this same spot. In fact, Matt used the same gesture, like a karate chop, every time he said it in that same spot.

"If the defendant corporation cared more about people, it would have followed Dr. Caughlin's advice ten years ago, to put fire retardant into the material. But that was too expensive. And here sits Jackie Ann, misshapen for life. Here sits Jackie Ann, the monster no one will look at. Here sits Jackie Ann, the victim of corporate profit and greed."

Two of the jurors glanced at one another. Matt had seen them having lunch together each day of the trial in the cafeteria. A bond must exist there. The timing of their glance told him they had discussed his theme and were down with it.

"Jackie Ann did not sit through the trial because her doctors advised against it. They told you that reliving the event that changed her life would be devastating to her psychological state.

"They told you that hearing the doctors talk about her future could impact her dedication to rehabilitation. They told you she could not sit for long periods of more than fifteen minutes."

Juror Three looked over at the plaintiff. She could not bear it. She wanted to stare. It was horrible to want that, but she felt compelled. She looked again.

Jackie Ann felt the juror looking at her. She had developed a sixth sense for that in the last two years. Juror Three recalled Jackie Ann's testimony about this and stopped staring at the plaintiff.

"Now, since I have to cover this same material, I am asking Jackie Ann to leave the courtroom until you return your verdict. Jackie Ann, will you please step outside?" the litigator asked his client. Jackie Ann quietly rose and left the courtroom.

Matt had told a white lie. He would not cover the same material. The jury had it in mind. Yet his mention of it stirred an anticipatory emotional response as they watched Jackie Ann leave the courtroom. It was bad enough seeing her. Now they had to hear her lawyer cover the expert testimony in its gruesome detail?

Juror Four wanted to leave. He recalled the testimony about the skin grafts, about the debriding, about the scabbing. He wondered if he would be forced to see the hospital photographs again. *Oh, god*, he thought.

The renewed image trapped in each juror's mind, Matt had sealed the question of damages. During jury selection, each juror had promised to fairly compensate the plaintiff sight unseen. Then, Matt had asked the judge to allow his client to enter, so the venire could see her for a moment. The judge nodded, and Matt walked to the back of the courtroom, opened the door, and summoned the plaintiff. Muffled sounds echoed around the courtroom as the potential jurors faced the damaged goods for the first time. Matt walked her to the center of the courtroom and asked the judge if she could disrobe. "Your honor, she has a bikini on underneath for this purpose."

"Objection. This is becoming a spectacle, your honor. This is highly prejudicial to the defense. And evidence has not even begun to be presented. We are in voir dire!" Justin Cobb stood at the defense table in a gray suit, behind gray spectacles, staring sincerely at the judge.

"Mr. Lambert?"

"It is important the potential jurors understand the burns and their severity before they can honestly commit to returning a fair verdict if they find liability."

"Sustained. You may exit the courtroom Ms. Sader," invited the judge. Cobb proudly sat down. Matt had to turn away to avoid smiling. Jackie Ann wasn't wearing a bikini. Cobb's objection maddened the potential jurors, who now had to resort to mental imagery, which would bring into their minds images far worse than had she disrobed. And by objecting, Cobb had corroborated the imagery. Cobb might as well have said, "Your honor, it is too ugly to imagine."

But imagine they did. If the body was half as bad as the face and arms, good lord, thought one of the potential jurors. One raised her hand and asked to be excused, holding her other hand to her mouth, as if about to vomit. Judge Dixon excused this person after a sidebar with counsel.

Matt called Jackie Ann to the stand on day three, at the end of the day. He timed it so she would be done by five o'clock, the judge's long-established quitting time. He covered the fire and how it started and how she became exposed to it. He quickly showed through her eyes the horror of being engulfed in a burning pantsuit, with material that made the fire burn hotter than had she been standing naked in the fire itself.

The jury envisioned how the scarring came to be. They saw the stark hospital photographs Jackie Ann authenticated, painstakingly, as Matt passed them into the jury box.

After that, Cobb did not even touch her. "Pass the witness," the old war horse called out when it was his turn. Impressive move, thought Matt, and he wondered how Cobb had fallen for the bikini routine.

Now he had them in closing argument. They had seen her briefly, and Matt had once again taken the damaged goods away from them. The image remained fixed in their minds at the conscious and unconscious levels. Matt knew that he had won over the emotional side of the jurors. Now he had to close the door on their conscious minds. He worked his corporate greed theme.

"The in-house expert at Daycon Enterprises told the vice president of manufacturing that given the content of this material, without retardant, it would ignite and burn. The vice president's email to the CEO repeated this advice. What did these men do? Did they add retardant? Did they say, 'Oh, well then, let's find another material?' You know what they did. And because of their decision, Jackie Ann is a victim for life."

He stepped back to the secret spot, and with his little karate chop said softly, "A victim of corporate greed. A victim of putting sales above safety. A victim of reckless decision making."

Juror Eight wondered how long Matt would go on. He wanted to hear Cobb take on this mess and clean it up. Eight liked Cobb. Cobb looked at Eight whenever he was making an important point during his examination of the witnesses. This plaintiff's lawyer made him sick. "Jackie Ann" this and "Jackie Ann" that. She never should have strayed near the fire. If she hadn't, Juror Eight thought to himself, we would not have had to sit her for two weeks listening to this shit. He could not wait for deliberations, where he would be just like Cobb.

"And that, ladies and gentlemen, is why you are here. What will it take to compensate Jackie Ann for being burned? What will it take to replace the life she would have had? What will it take to provide some measure of security for her life expectancy of forty years?"

Matt did not want to open the door anymore on damages. Old Cobb would feast inside that room if he could get in.

"Jackie Ann puts it in your hands. Take your time, ladies and gentlemen. This vote will be the most important one in Jackie Ann's life. She wants you to take care, review the evidence, and take the time you need to determine a fair verdict and reasonable compensation. We will wait for you as long as it takes." Matt turned and walked away to his seat.

"Mr. Cobb, you may now make your closing statement."

"This is a sad case, but it is sad because this nice lady was not careful. She stepped that extra step to peer into the fire pit. She stepped that last step that caused her to come on fire. She stepped that last step to destroy herself. She now steps before you and wants a lot of money for her mistake. You are like the fire. Do not let her step closer. Because awarding her damages will be the true thing to destroy her life. She is working and self-sufficient. She is engaged to a nice man. She is capable of having beautiful children. She is not out of pocket one dime. You are the fire. By giving her the money, you will be creating another free ride in our society, a society that needs people like her working and struggling like all of us do every day of our lives. Her mistake should not equate to a free ride for her."

*Go baby go*, thought Juror Eight. *That's my main man, Mr. Cobb. I can use that mojo in the jury room.* Juror Eight was on fire. The other jurors were listening, too.

"Corporate greed? Mr. Lambert's emotional appeal is like the fire that started this whole thing. And it too should be doused. Throw the water bucket of truth and logic on it. Put it out right now."

Juror One shifted in his seat again.

"You heard the executives testify that they had differing opinions. And you heard Dr. Caughlin admit on cross-examination that his tests were not conclusive but only preliminary. Dr. Caughlin also lied about his credentials. And remember the graduate thesis? Yes, you remember, the one I got him to admit he plagiarized! Can he be believed here? Could he be believed by Daycon's vice president of marketing? Could he be believed by Daycon's CEO? For all we know, putting the costly retardant into the material would have been a waste of money."

*Slam*, thought Juror Eight. *My man, my man, my man.* Eight wanted to high five old Cobbles right now. The two jurors who ate lunch together glanced odd looks at one another.

"And so, ladies and gentlemen, Mr. Lambert and Ms. Sader have put on a wonderful show for us. I hope you were entertained. But this is serious business. Do not award her a dime. Thank you."

The aged litigator strode to his seat certain he had put the nail in Lambert's coffin.

Lambert wanted to throw up. Cobb had smoked that one. What to do?

"Mr. Lambert? Rebuttal, if you wish," said Judge Dixon from the bench. Lambert's ears were ringing, and Dixon sounded like he was whispering from the end of a tunnel.

"Mr. Lambert?" Dixon raised his voice, with a tone as if to say, 'Know when to quit, kid.' Lambert had just had his head clobbered in and now he was expected to 'rebut' the old man?

Matt mustered strength he did not have and rose. He stayed at the table and turned to the jurors.

"Dr. Caughlin made some mistakes. But the evidence is undisputed that he told the vice president that his testing showed that the retardant would diminish the flammability by at least forty percent. And you heard our expert in materials testify that based on his examination of the remnants in this case, the degree of inflammable fiber in Jackie Ann's pantsuit would have, to a reasonable degree of scientific certainty, prevented her clothes from catching on fire, and, even if they did catch on fire, her rolling on the ground as she did would have extinguished the flames before they reached the skin.

"Jackie Ann was three feet from the fire pit when the ember burst unexpectedly. She was standing no closer than the others around the backyard fire pit, having cocktails before a lovely barbeque. That warm summer evening became an inferno for Jackie Ann, changing her life in seconds. She cannot go back to that backyard. She fears fire and heat of any sort. She relives rolling on the ground on fire, panicking in horror as it got hotter and hotter. She will relive that suffering for the rest of her life."

Juror Eight wanted to throw something. He imagined a trap door under Lambert and pushing the button to open it. That would take his white ass down.

The lunchtime jurors exchanged glances. He had them back on track.

"We all have bills to pay. Daycon has a big bill to pay. It took away the life of Jackie Ann Sader as she knew it. What that bill will be is your decision. Hold Daycon accountable. Hold Daycon responsible. Hold Daycon to a higher standard of safety than its bottom line. Take your time, and we will patiently await your justice."

Cobb's face was somber. His company representative whispered into his ear. Cobb wanted to swat the noise away. He had the jurors in his hand and this little boy of a lawyer just upstaged him with the last word.

"Ladies and gentlemen of the jury, the bailiff will escort you to the jury room for your deliberations. Once you have reached a verdict, tell the bailiff." Dixon loved hotly contested cases, and he had one here. It was a grueling two weeks, but it was over.

He slammed the gavel. "Court is in recess," he declared and stomped off the bench and withdrew into his chambers.

## The Barrister

The winter snow I do not bash,
for each new downfall brings me cash,
as drivers on the frozen roads
will often cause their cars to crash;

while in my office I await,
a spider that negotiates,
unless my demands they spuriously spurn
with offers not commensurate

then into a lion I'll turn,
and litigate 'til all Hell burns;
don't blame me for this happenstance,
as some lessons are never learned.

The summer rain I do not bash,
as each new downfall brings me cash,
as drivers on the wetted roads,
will often cause their cars to crash.

*—John Lambremont, Sr.*

# OLD SOLDIERS

RANDALL PATTERSON

The mediator is saying, "An old lawyer told me early on in my career—" (he's about my age) "—'Bobby, if you stay with these ol' lawsuits for any length of time, you will sooner or later come to the point that you are suspicious of ever'thing. You'll no longer believe alleged injuries exist, and you'll have serious doubts about a person's death.'" And he turns his attention to me. I turn my face to the window. This is his way of telling me I'm stupid and that I ought to offer the plaintiff more money. Turning my face to the window is my way of telling him to go fuck himself.

Howard puts his hand on my wrist in what I think, frankly, is too controlling and too condescending a manner for a guy I'm paying to sit here and shut up while I do all the work. I hate defense attorneys. They always think they're the ones in charge when, as presiding insurance company hack, I hold the gold and the gold is what's sold, no matter how much talking they want to do. I take a nice long look at my wrist and now turn my face back to the window, but Howard doesn't read sign language any better than Bobby does.

Howard, responding solely to the mediator—since lawyers acknowledge no one but each other until it's time to get paid—chuckles politely and begins the retelling of an unrelated old war story. "Well, a-Bobby, let me tell you about something that happened to me many a moon ago. Why, I once had me an ol' case, a bad ol' case . . ."

That's his way. I notice that, for a litigator, he doesn't seem to like a lot of conflict, although I guess his style works well enough for him. One of these smooth operator types in the courtroom, never gets upset, barely ever objects. In fact, you can barely even see him. It's either a style or he's just getting old. Personally, I have the feeling he might have been a much different kind of lawyer twenty or thirty years ago when he first started getting hired. But his record is probably no different from the record of any lawyer who has no say over which cases he takes to trial. Sometimes he wins them and sometimes he loses them, but at least sometimes he wins them. And, for the most part, the ones he loses never should have been tried in the first place. They should have been settled. Like this one, for instance. I know it's a stupid theory of negligence they have against us, but Jesus Christ the woman almost died. The worse the injury is, the less a jury cares about fault. They just want to help. But try to tell that to an insurance company bureaucrat like my boss Leonard.

Leonard. Sometimes Leonard's right, and sometimes Leonard's wrong. More precisely, he's almost always wrong, but sometimes the results he gets don't prove it. I remember seeing one of those courtroom dramas on TV one time. I remember what I recall being the opening scene, wherein a completely ruined plaintiff is wheeled into the courtroom, drooling and angelic, profoundly brain damaged by whatever accident he was involved in, and I turned to my wife and I said, "Kathy, the problem is, this scene is completely unbelievable. No defendant would try this case. No insurance carrier would be that idiotic." She said, "We don't even know what the facts are," and I said, "The facts are that guy is fucked up."

Enter Leonard and fast forward to the Nguyen trial about a year ago. Seven-year-old paraplegic. Plaintiff attorneys show a day-in-the-life video of this poor little kid catheterizing himself and dragging himself around his crummy house to get from toy to toy. Neuropsychiatrists and pediatric urologists and orthopedists testify that he'll never walk again, that it will cost five million dollars just to stay the way he is (that no amount of money will ever make him any better), that if he forgets to lift himself every twenty minutes to keep the blood circulating they'll end up cutting off his legs, and that if he ever has sex it will only be by way of a series of strange fanatical maneuvers and injections into the penis and that he still won't have any sensation. They testify that there's a scraping procedure and other worse procedures that may elicit a viable spermatozoa for use in in-vitro fertilization. I begged that idiot Leonard to let me settle the case for two and a half million, knowing our exposure was up to five times that. When the jury came back, we paid nothing.

A few months ago was the Wreath case. Leonard wouldn't settle that one for chump change because, after his usual strenuous analysis, he concluded that the case was 'bullshit.' Employer driving his employee home, employee didn't have his seatbelt on and failed to shut the door. Guy turns a corner, employee spills out, plaintiff widow alleges gross negligence for the failure to train, as if her husband had come across no other opportunity in life to learn to shut the door and wear a seatbelt. Jury award: six million.

We may as well use Howard as anybody on this case. He wins some of them. He loses some of them. He's going to lose this one. He's going to lose this one big, and there's nothing I can do about it and there's nothing he can do about it, either, since Leonard won't give us enough money to settle it. If he were at the top of his game, if he were the sharpest shyster in the state, there would be nothing he could do to win this case short of knocking off all the lawyers on the other side, and there are plenty of them, too. That firm has brought out all the big guns for this one. Well-connected guns. One of them is known to play golf with the judge. I suppose we're to believe they haven't had discussions about this case. The plaintiff firm is, of course, also a huge contributor to his election campaigns. In these rural venues, they're all kissing cousins. And we're strolling in there all the way from Houston to try to tell them how things are supposed to be done. We may as well be wearing Fuck the Judge T-shirts when we walk in there for opening statements. We may as well be wearing Fuck the Jury T-shirts while we're at it.

So, why not use Howard? Why not? In fact, why not use the worst lawyer we've ever met, way past his prime, mumbling his arguments to the jury, scratching his balls, burping whiskey breath at them, flirting with the women? Flirting with the *men*? Flirting with *the judge while we're at it*? Why not hire someone with Tourette Syndrome who may at best be able to disorient the jury so completely that they no longer understand what we're arguing about?

Howard will be just fine.

Of course, I suppose there's the slightest chance we might be able to settle it for fifty thousand dollars. I think I'll forget the instruction Leonard gave me to 'Tell them if they want fifty thousand and a penny, they can suck the turds right out of my ass!' I think I'll forget I ever heard him say that. I know Howard has forgotten it. Although Howard probably *really has* forgotten it, old as he is.

Jesus, I wonder how old Howard really is. It's his little three-man firm so no one's going to make him retire. He refers to his partner as 'the youngster,' and he's ten years older than me, and I'm practically tottering at the grave myself. I suppose I could rely on the possibility that we'll get a jury of *our* peers rather than peers of the parties to the suit. Maybe we'll get a jury of disgruntled middle-aged adolescents in love with girls from the clerical unit whom they've never even kissed. Maybe we'll get a bunch of old lawyers who can no longer match their left shoes to their right, which is something I don't even want to bring up to Howard for fear it will lower his self-confidence.

The mediator walks out of the room after laughing politely at Howard's old war story. As I see the reflection of the door close behind him in the window, I turn my head again to face the others.

Rudy says, "What do you think we should do, boss?" He has his pen poised over his paper. I probably don't really need to be here to supervise him but it does get me out of the office.

I ask him, "Where are we?"

He looks back down at his notebook. "They're at two million, eight hundred and fifty thousand, and we're at thirty thousand."

"Go up another five? Is that what you think, Howard?"

Howard takes a long whistling breath through hairy old misshapen nostrils and leans back in his chair. He knits his brows together and purses his lips, as if what he's going to say could change the course of Leonard. Finally, his posture collapses a little and he mumbles, "Well, I don't know what else we *can* do. Shit, Warren, if we only got fifty grand, then we only got fifty grand, and it's a-gonna be hard to make that amount of money *stretch*. Now look, I know what you're a-gonna say to me, I *think*, but I've got a client in this here dogfight and I've got to say my piece nonetheless. And what I've a-got to say . . . izzzzz . . . that I still think y'all ought to think about offering a little bit more money on this ol' thing. Or a lot. Because you know this girl's pretty bad hurt. Hell, I'll say it. She's *bad* hurt, and the jury's going to respond to that."

"I know, Howard. I've already talked to Burt about it. He said we can call him for more money when we get ten thousand apart. Then he'll talk to Leonard."

I don't know if the sound he makes is a laugh or the suppression of some other thing. "Ten thousand apart," he says. "Ten thousand dollars, you're saying."

"Mmmm."

Rudy's head is swiveling back and forth to see mine, to see Howard's, to see mine. He says, as a neophyte sometimes will, "Then, let's try to determine what Leonard was thinking. I mean, he's the big boss for a reason, right?"

Rudy's probably bucking for my job. Sometimes I think he can have it.

Howard nips it. "He wasn't, son. He wasn't thinking. Know that."

Rudy gives him a look, and I say to Rudy, "It's a very bad liability case the plaintiff has. That's what Leonard sees. However, it's a very good damages case the plaintiff has. That, he doesn't seem to see. And the better the damages case is, the less good the liability case needs to be for the plaintiff to hit his jackpot."

"But first he has to prove liability."

"Theoretically. Yes."

"I can see what Leonard's thinking," he goes on. "I can see how he's right."

I look at Howard and say in a lazy voice nobody sensible would believe, "He might be."

"But if the jurors don't follow the law . . . ? Right?"

"There's going to be some evidence of liability. There will be a fact question. They say we were parked the wrong way on the side of the road. We were. They say that's negligence, per se. It is. But you still have to find causation. That's where you get the fact question. Is our guy parking on the shoulder facing the wrong way what caused this stupid bitch to pull out onto the highway when she couldn't see? Fact question. Means it's up to the jury to decide. The jury can make the wrong decision if they want to . . . And, let me tell you, when they see that googly eyed brain-damaged bitch walk in there and ask them for a lot of money, that's exactly what they'll do." I turn now to Howard, who at least knows something, and I say, "I've gotten to where I hate these things."

He shakes his head clear of the thought and leans back in the chair again. "Ohhhhhhhhhh, I enjoy a good mediation still. I enjoy the game. Well, hell, it's a real good game as long as I've got something to work with. Not like this one, of course. Lord, son, they got me where I'm a-trying to play a game of poker with a deck of tarot cards. I'm trying to punt the ball right now without a foot. They got me playing craps with a pair of goddamn knuckle-bones, with a handful of some goddamn chicken feet and beads and a piece of old floss, and when it hits it—the fan, that is—the shit, I'm saying— they'll be a-saying they can't figure out why I'm a-not a-winning."

I nod. "They'll say it. They'll say, 'I thought Howard was a *good* lawyer.'"

"They will?"

I avert my eyes. "They've said it before."

He looks at me with something approaching horror at the inanity of this world, and he almost says something about reasonableness or common sense probably, but his jaw snaps shut helplessly instead, and he just sits there staring into space.

There isn't much I can say to him. He's done work for Leonard before. What was he expecting? I shrug and offer, "At least the mediator's providing lunch."

He seems satisfied to change the subject. The muscles in his cheeks suddenly loosen, and he stops grinding his teeth, and he says, "Yep, that's another thing. Pay a sumbitch eight hundred dollars a side and you might expect more than to get a bologna sandwich from down the street by one o'clock."

Rudy inserts, "How long have you been a supervisor, Warren?"

"About a year."

"How long did it take you?"

"About thirty-seven years."

Howard snorts at this and leans back in his chair. Rudy looks at me quietly and says, "How long have you been at *this* company?"

"I don't know. Few years. Four, maybe. Three and change."

"I'm happy to be here, myself. You should see the last place I was. I know you're not supposed to talk to bosses about past employers but . . . I'll just say I'm glad to be where I am."

"Yeah, I can well imagine. It's a good job for a claims adjuster. Very good. And you've got one of the worst jobs in the office, too, and it's still better than any other claims job you'll ever have."

"I think you're right. So far, you are . . . and I'd have no reason to leave."

*Nice save*, I think. "Before they made me a supervisor, I was doing basically your desk. Some heavy stuff and some light stuff. So, like you, I was always having to change gears. One minute, screwing around with some guy who won't accept a used bumper. The next minute, trying to figure out whether some asshole's really brain damaged or not. My office was just a closet with my name on it, but it beat the shit out of the cubicle I'd come from."

"No kidding."

He seems to be asking me something, and I don't know what it is. I try, "Well, Rudy, you're doing just fine."

"I am?"

"Sure."

"I want to do well. I want to move up when I can. I know it's a matter of timing, of being in the right place at the right time and all of that."

"There's that, yes."

"You can do a great job, and if they don't need any more supervisors, then they don't need any more supervisors, right?"

I want to say, 'You can do a great job and find yourself feet up in a dumpster,' but I don't. Instead I say, "Uh-huh."

So he wants to move up the corporate ladder, such as it is. I'm wondering whether he shaves yet.

A lesser man, of course, would never admit the possibility of the obvious. I do know that he makes it sound like a lot of fun to be young and potentially brilliant with a good attitude and what appears to be an attractiveness to women. What is this feeling I have toward him, then? Should I call it 'hatred' exactly? The specific reaction I am having is more complex, possibly, than what might be casually termed 'hatred,' although 'hatred' will certainly do as a category. And why do I feel this way? Could it by any stretch of the imagination be due to his relative youth and comparable brilliance? Or to my relative age and fading vocabulary? As long as he does his work, I guess, and stays out of my thinning hair, I have no particular reason to have him killed. I mean, nothing out of the ordinary. I mean, nothing I haven't already considered.

Rudy pushes his chair away from the table and says, "Bathroom."

The door closes behind him and Howard says, "How's the new boy working out? Is he new?"

"Rudy?" I shrug. "I guess he's working out. I don't know. He's a warm body. His hand can push a piece of paper across a desk. He can do as well as anybody to settle a two million dollar case for fifty thousand dollars."

"Ain't that the truth. Well, it's a dog's world, boy. Not a man in it. Not a man."

We sit looking at each other and out the window and at the desk, and he adds, "Reckon he's off somewhere calling Leonard to tell him how he's getting badmouthed over here?"

"I don't think so. He's new. He's probably still reasonably scared enough of me not to do that."

"Maybe we ought to hope so. I didn't mean to go on and on like I did . . . Did I go on and on?"

"A little. I don't care."

He leans back in his chair and puts a toothpick in his mouth. "Yahh. It's like you said, boy. This day is all about a bologna sandwich by noontime. It's not about anything else."

We sit barely hating each other for a moment, tied together by a hatred for something else, and I feel close enough to him in this foxhole to bother to ask, "So, how's *your* thing going? Are they giving you any cases?"

"Awww, you know I appreciate the work, but I wouldn't make a living off you boys' company. Not my only client. Besides, I'm kind of trying to slowly shut this ol' thing down. I been at it a real long time, you know. The only thing I really keep it open for anymore is my partner Chipper. Have you ever met Chipper?"

I pause. "Yeah, I've bumped into him, Howard."

He pauses longer. "Oh well hell that's right. Y'all worked real close together on that damn oil well injury, that drill rig injury didn't you?"

"No, it was an auto accident."

"Well, that's what it was," he says and turns to see Rudy walk back in and tell us he saw the mediator in the hall and gave him the additional five thousand.

I don't turn around from the window. I look at his reflection as his reflection looks at the back of my head, and I say, "How'd he respond?"

"Not too well, I don't think."

"I always say you haven't done your job unless the mediator's mad at you by lunchtime."

"You don't think we can get any more money to try to settle it?"

"I don't think we can, no."

"Do we want to try?"

I shrug. "Give Burt a call. Ask him if he wants to talk to Leonard."

Rudy nods his head with such optimistic fury that I would know it to be sarcasm if it were anybody else, but Rudy is young, credulous, interested, a real go-getter, just the kind of asshole I probably was at his age. He must be thinking to himself, 'I know I can! I know I can!' as he so eagerly punches numbers on his cell phone even before he walks out of the room. There are so many terrible things to think about this situation, and this child's Pollyanna attitude toward it, that I think I'll just look out the window rather than contemplate them all. The worst of these bad things is that he'll begin to understand them himself over time and will be eaten by them, changed, or that over time, I'll end up working for him. Or both. Yeah, that's it. It's probably both.

## Pled

Your client's deposition, and an omission
never revealed has jaggedly surfaced. Now
the conference room's walls buckle and duck,
halving themselves like the taking of sides
in a schoolyard fight. The defense attorney is so joyous
she frowns bitterly as masquerade. You fume
gaseous, the calculated implosion, the knowing
toying, another's bonanza. As though
you just learned you'd been switched at birth.
After hours you school your client—dumpsters
in backlots containing company garbage
contain company property—yet,
he only thinks he's stolen.

Everyone recalls the pageant of your activist wife,
her unperfumed huff, delivering your dinner
to the office. She spoke to no one, tossed the hot
frozen dinner tray atop your desk, other people's problems
on paper beneath the dripping gravy, her statement made.
The day you know the instant case is all but lost
she files her own petition.

When night comes, night itself turning
its back at one long confederacy,
you roam through thick blue and gray texts,
seeking the song of law where it levels,
raking out not the answer but the match,
every page you turn returns your argument to you
as your own countenance weathers like the desert hills,
as if you were shepardizing the laws of Moses,
where all is sound, the elements menacing
and the faintest bereft wail is a chime of enunciation.

—*Cynthia Schwartzberg Edlow*

# SERVES YOU RIGHT

## JACK EWING

Six years on the job, and you still sweat out the first call: It sets the tone for the day. What's behind Door Number One?

Recheck name and address: Yep, this is the place, a shabby frame bungalow, identical to a dozen others along the street. White paint flakes away around Venetian-blinded windows. Screen door contains enough holes in the mesh to admit an army of insects. Knock with your right hand. Keep the left behind your back.

After a moment, the door opens. A tiny gray-haired lady in a faded print dress and orthopedic shoes pushes the screen at you. "Yes?" She blinks into bright sunlight.

Keep an eye out for a weapon on her, remembering the hag with a hatpin a couple years back. "Leora Rains?"

"Yes, I am." Her smile reveals too-white teeth, too-pink gums.

"This is for you." Bring the folded paper forward and place it in her age-spotted hand.

She adjusts bifocals and reads her name on the front where it says DEFENDANT. She stares at the fancy lettering then looks up, eyebrows coming together. "What is it?"

"Summons and Complaint, Mrs. Rains." Check the copy in the pocket of your summer-weight jacket. "You owe Downtown Med Center four thousand nine hundred and eighty-three bucks and change. Didn't you hear from Gleed and Crown, the collection attorneys, about this?"

"Yes, I received some letters." Her gaze fixes on the paper in her hand. "But I threw them away."

Some people are just too dumb for words. "Why'd you do that?"

"I was sure health insurance covered my operation."

Silently, you wonder what doctors took out or put in. Maybe they removed her brain. Must have—she ignored Gleed and Crown.

Her wrinkles deepen, her voice quavers. "How can this be?" The summons wobbles in bony fingers that are all blue veins.

You say, as instructed: "I just hand out papers. Thing to do is call the lawyers. Number's on the back." Show her. "Call within thirty days or they'll take you to court to get the money."

"I don't have a phone!" Her eyes beg for sympathy.

"Use a neighbor's. Or write the lawyers. Get in touch soon."

Mrs. Rains protests she doesn't get around so good. Her husband's dead. She doesn't know where she'll dredge up that kind of cash. She barely gets by on Social Security. Her voice climbs on the Shrill-O-Meter. Before she starts crying, cut her off. You've heard it all before, hundreds of times, every excuse in the book. Even if you feel a little sorry for some, like this old lady, what are you supposed to do? Pay the bills for them? "Look, talk to the lawyers. They'll set up a payment schedule."

Leave her standing there, like something carved out of soap. Walk back to the car, a block down. A black sedan, it goes with your dark suit. Together, they lend an official look, an edge in the low-rent districts where you often work.

Climbing in, you get the AC going and fill out the turn-in form attached to your copy of the summons. There are spaces to write in name of person served, address, date, time, and thumbnail ID: race, hair and eye color, approximate age, weight, and height. The form is intended to check the process server's honesty, to discourage claiming successful service and collecting the fee—when actually you've gone nowhere near the defendant's house and have trashed his paper to save bother.

You'd never do such a thing, of course, but other less scrupulous members of the trade might. A guy in the next county got in hot water for putting down the "Chris Smith" he served as a white male, forty, five-foot nine, one hundred and fifty pounds. Problem was, the real defendant was a twenty-something black female named Christine, about six two and three hundred pounds.

Sign the completed form, swearing it's true, and toss it in the glove box. One down, thirty-some to go, all arranged in geographical order—except for one purposely left on the bottom—so you can hit them efficiently. But you'll still cover sixty, seventy miles driving about a city sweltering in the grip of summer. It's going to be a busy day, and at a minimum twenty-five dollars per deadbeat, plus mileage, potentially a profitable one.

Money's the only reason to stick with it. Wherever you go, you aren't welcome. Customers in gated estates, condos and hi-rises, suburban ranchers, bungalows and split-levels, ghetto shacks, tenements, and flops all hate you for bringing bad news. And you hate them all right back with equal intensity—regardless of race, creed, color, national origin, or income—for the contempt that shows in their eyes. It's a dirty job, but somebody's got to do it. Pity the poor guy next in line behind you, repossessing cars and couches and big-screen TV sets.

Next victim is a squat pot-bellied, middle-aged white man in a sleeveless gray T-shirt with underarm sweat stains the size of dinner plates. He looks and smells like he was baptized in beer and has been swilling it nonstop ever since.

"Yeah?" He gives you the fisheye from the doorway of a dinky rented room.

"Nile Sledge?"

"So?" Nile scratches three-day stubble and hitches baggy pants.

"I'm here to give you this." Whip out the paper, stick it in his hand, step back.

Mr. Sledge stares stupidly before realizing what it is. He works himself into a huff in a half-minute. Purple-faced and panting curses, he tears the summons into tiny pieces and flings them after you. He slams the door, still airing his four-letter-word collection.

It all rolls off like rain off a Turtle Wax shine. Long as they throw nothing but words and paper, who cares? The lucky recipient can wipe his butt with it, for all the good it will do. You'll still get paid. And the lawyers will still hound him.

Sylvia Maybon is a blowsy blonde, made up like a Kewpie doll, with lots of detailing around her eyes and mouth. She wears a frilly robe that falls open when she reaches to take the summons. "Oops." She tucks back a rosy-tipped breast the size of a California grapefruit and nibbles a corner of the paper, eyes locked on yours. "Thank you." She closes the door with both hands. Her robe parts again, giving a full-length view.

You say: "No, thank *you*."

When Scott Schmidt, a young fellow with connect-the-dot pimples, opens the door, you see a closet-sized room behind him. His teen-aged bride sits in a ratty armchair, the only furniture visible, taping a disposable diaper onto a baby squirming on her lap. Mr. Schmidt is naive enough to tell you where he works. This tidbit gives the lawyers a potential source of income, if garnishing becomes necessary. It also earns you a bonus for providing the tip.

Joe Franks is a heavy-set, weary-looking guy. He doesn't say word one when you serve him at his tire store.

Lisa Stillwater, an anorexic ad agency receptionist, glares through rhinestone-encrusted eyeglasses and calls you a bunch of bad names. Some might even be true.

Simon Klein's skinny, pinch-faced wife leads you to his bedroom where he's plugged into some machine with tubes running under the covers. His eyes are glassy, his face made of wax. He barely has strength to lift a mummy's hand and take the summons.

Marta Ramirez is a fat Hispanic woman with six snot-nosed kids making racket behind her. She lives in a rundown project that smells like it's survived a recent fire. "Que?" Her unibrow twists as she turns the paper this way and that. "Que?"

There's always one who won't admit she's who you know she is.

You ring the doorbell of a tidy frame house. When the door opens on a chubby, forty-something woman trying to look thirty, you ask: "Colleen Qualls?"

"What is it?"

"Are you Colleen Qualls?"

"Who wants to know?"

"I've got something for Colleen Qualls. You her?"

"Can't you tell me what it is?"

"Not unless you're Colleen."

"Why? Is it a secret or something?"

"Let's say it's a surprise."

Her heavily shadowed eyes light up. She brushes at a lacquered curl that springs back into place. "I love surprises. Give me a hint."

"Okay. Maybe I'm from the lottery commission with a check for

Colleen. Maybe I found something she lost."

Her face goes through a series of changes, starting with hope and ending with suspicion. "Maybe you're full of crap." She shuts the door in your face, looking as though she wants to bite you.

You break for lunch at a fast-food joint, eager to plow through the day's chaff and get to the kernel: the paper at the bottom of the pile. After a tasteless burger and bitter iced tea, you're ready for the south side, the rough side of town.

Next target: Oscar Petty, who works at Ace's Barber Shop. The place is sandwiched between a porn store and a bar. You stroll in, the comforting weight of a roll of nickels in your pocket. It's a hedge against the only real difference between the rich and the poor: People with nothing to lose are less predictable in adversity.

To the right, four young black dudes wearing mirrored shades slouch in high-backed chairs. You feel their eyes as you approach the first of two barbers: a tall, thin, light-skinned guy running electric clippers over a teen's gourd-shaped head.

You say to him, "Excuse me, Oscar here?"

He waves clippers toward the back. You start that way, passing the other barber, a dark man built like a football lineman. He's using a straight-edged razor to give sidewalls to an elderly black gentleman asleep in the chair. The second barber doesn't say anything but tracks you without moving his head.

A small, chocolate-colored man with graying hair emerges from a room in the rear of the shop. He wears coveralls and carries a push broom and dustpan. Ask him: "You Oscar Petty?"

He looks at your mouth. The whites of his eyes are bloodshot and yellowish, like Tabasco-laced egg yolks. He nods.

"Can I speak in private with you a sec?"

He props his tools against a wall, shuffles toward the front door. You follow him away from silver-eyed customers and wooden-faced barbers. Ten feet from the shop the little man faces you, eyes fixed on the knot of your tie. Pull out the paper.

"Mr. Petty, I'm here to deliver this sum—"

The shop door opens, and the larger barber glides over. He holds the open razor in a fist the size of a coconut. Sunlight glints off the foam-flecked blade. "*Don't* give him that." His voice is soft and low. Over his breast pocket, at eye level, is embroidered ACE.

Take a step back, heels crunching broken glass, give him the line: "Sir, I'm a duly empowered process server, legally serving this paper, and—"

"Don't *give* him that," Ace whispers. His breath is all minty.

Take another backward step, aware of faces pressed against insides of shop windows and gathered along the sidewalk to watch.

A dark fat man with a pool cue steps out of the bar. Beside him, a tall, slender guy shifts his grip on a beer bottle.

A young man with acne stands at the porn shop door, slick magazine open to a photo showing a black male and a white female engaged in an act that would have been cause for lynching a few decades back.

Two little girls with jump ropes, pigtailed hair done up in dozens of bright bows, pause a yard away.

"Is whitey gonna get cut?" one asks.

"Look like it," the other says matter-of-factly.

Talk fast to the barber. "You don't understand, Mr. . . . . Ace. This is a summons and complaint. Says Mr. Petty owes somebody money." Sweat gathers in the wings of your nose and in the hollow above your upper lip. Your shirt sticks to your back. "I'm not here to collect cash."

Wave the paper, your other hand tight and damp about two dollars' worth of nickels. "Just delivering bills, like the mailman." Try on a grin, wondering what your lips are really doing.

Ace leans forward from the waist, like a building about to fall. You look from Ace to Oscar. The little man stares at the sidewalk as though the ground is about to open up. He doesn't say zip.

Give it one last try. "Believe me, brother," you say to the barber, "if I don't hand him this paper today, the sheriff will bring it later. It'll mean more hassle. And it'll cost Oscar more in the end."

"Don't give him *that*." Ace flicks the razor. A glob of lime-scented shaving cream lands on your cheek. An inch closer, the flashing blade would have laid a deep slice there.

The little girls laugh.

"Go away." Ace forms the words carefully with thick lips.

You go. Let the law fool with them.

The rest of the afternoon, you meet with varying success, but nab quite a few defendants in the early evening, around dinnertime.

Finally, there's only one summons unaccounted for. The one you always save for last, like dessert. The one with the name on it almost as familiar as your own: Brent Wixom.

You'd been given Wixom's paper long ago, when you first began as a process server, when you still felt bad about bringing people legal misery, when he only owed a few hundred to a loan company. You've dogged his trail since, following him to dozens of ramshackle dwellings scattered about the city and surrounding suburbs. Each time, the amount of his debt grew, thanks to lawyers' fees and interest. Now, instead of hundreds, he owes thousands. You'd find his latest address. He'd be gone. You'd dig up new leads:

From a former next-door neighbor, a white-haired man with an educated manner, still living in half of the duplex Wixom once rented: "Brent hasn't lived here in months. He once mentioned moving in with a friend on Columbus Avenue."

From the landlord of a fleabag walk-up, a gaunt little guy with suitcases under his eyes: "S.O.B. sneaked out in the middle of the night last December. Owed two months rent. Left beer cans and pizza boxes piled a foot deep, so roaches had a field day. Probably went to sponge off his sister, over in Parkview."

From a mail carrier with graying hair and a walrus moustache: "Here's the last address we got on him. Give me the ten spot."

You'd write down what you learned and turn in the papers for reprocessing. The lawyers would follow up through other channels, pin down a new number on a new street, and send you off again.

Slowly, you closed the gap. You'd started out more than a year behind him at the beginning. Now, the trail is only weeks old.

He'd been a blank at the start, too. Now, you know he's white, about thirty, six feet tall, slender, with short dark hair. Sure, that description could fit thousands of guys. But as you get closer, you've picked up a few other things to help identify the quarry.

He smokes filtered cigarettes. A sourpuss landlady mentions this, complaining about getting the smell out of drapes.

There's a mole at the base of his throat and a blue star tattoo on his right hand. These hints come from a former neighbor in a walk-up apartment building—a shapely redhead in tight T-shirt and jeans, she comes on to you like a pro while answering questions.

He drinks Schlitz beer and likes loud music, according to a rheumy old man with a room beneath one Wixom used to occupy.

You want this guy. It's a matter of professional pride to nail him.

You've gone after thousands of lowlife debtors and, outside of a couple who croaked or a handful that fled to other states, beyond reach, few have escaped service. Wixom won't get away, either, if you can help it. You've got a reputation to consider.

It's after nine when you pull up to Wixom's latest address. You coaxed it out of a balding blabbermouth who used to work with the man you're after, lubricating the guy with beer while posing as Wixom's long-lost buddy.

The place is on a country road five miles beyond city limits, but still in the county, in the trough of a shallow valley. It's a run-down, two-story clapboard house, blushed pink by the dying sun. You wonder if you've been steered wrong again by Wixom's chum, who maybe decoyed you out here long enough to make a call and give your prey time to escape from his real hideout to some other hole.

Might as well check it out, long as you're here. Park a hundred yards past the joint, behind a clump of brush that hides your car from the house, and walk back.

A light burns in the window. The door to the screened-in front porch is locked when you try it. Heavy metal music thumps inside.

Somebody lives here. Wixom?

Cat-foot it around the side of the house. In the driveway sits an old beat-up dark Ford. Jot down make and license plate number on the back of somebody's business card from your wallet, just in case. Might be worth extra dough.

At a side window on the first floor is a half-inch gap between the shade and the bottom of the sill. Put an eye to it.

Living room. A detergent commercial, sound dampened, plays on a TV set in one corner. In the middle of the room a scarred coffee table is piled with newspapers, empty takeout food containers, and

Schlitz cans. An arm's length away looms the back of an overstuffed chair. A hand with a lit filtered cigarette stuck between two fingers appears on the armrest of the chair, goes away again, chased by a cloud of exhaled smoke.

Hike around back. The veneer of the door here is peeling away in strips. Knock.

After a minute, a dim yellow bug light comes on overhead. The door opens a foot, letting out loud, so-called music. In lemony bulb glow the man with dark, shaggy hair seems the right age, the right height. His eyes narrow, sweep you up and down. "Who the hell are you?" There is surprise in his voice.

"Brent Wixom?"

The space between door and frame widens. He's wearing a tank top and denims. There's a dime-sized brown spot, like a drop of chocolate, where his neck meets the black mat of chest hair.

"How'd you find me?"

Moments like this, when you finally corner a slippery debtor, make the job worth it. Your voice is rich with satisfaction. "I've brought you something, Brent." Reach for the paper in your breast pocket.

His star-tattooed hand comes out from behind the door. "No, you don't!"

He points a finger at you: A finger that gleams, a finger with a hole in the end of it, a finger that roars as it catches fire.

You jackknife away but something slams you in the gut, lets air out, collapses you like a punctured balloon. Drop in a heap at his feet, clutching yourself, trying to hold back thick, warm liquid seeping between your fingers.

Wixom stands over you, gun aimed at your head. The bore looks big as a tunnel. "How do you like that, jerk? Thought you'd just waltz in and blast me, didn't you? Thought I wouldn't fight back, that I'd rabbit again? I'm through running. I'm going to the cops and tell them what I know. What do you think about that?"

What is he yapping about? You're drowning in a sea of sudden pain.

Wixom kicks you in the thigh with the toe of a sneaker. "What's the matter, big man, nothing to say? You mob guys all think you're tough. Don't look so tough now."

You want to tell him he's made a terrible mistake, that you're just a harmless process server, but you don't have the wind for it. Fumble with a bloody hand for the paper in your pocket.

"Don't try it." He jams the warm muzzle of the pistol against your temple and bends to slap your hand away. "I'll take the piece."

Feeling in your coat, Wixom finds nothing but the summons. He pats you down then unfolds the paper with his name on the front. He reads it, frowning, with frequent glances to make sure you won't pull anything. When he lowers the document, his eyes are two bleak holes in a white mask. "This is all you came about?" Doubt shreds his voice. "To give me a lousy summons?"

He leans, peers into your face. "Tony didn't send you out here to shut me up?"

You manage small nods and headshakes in response to his questions, trying not to moan in agony.

"Christ." Wixom runs shaky fingers through his hair. "I shot a damn process server. Now I'm really in trouble."

His eyes wander away and his body follows. "They'll put me in the lockup for this. I'm in deep tapioca. Be a sitting duck for Tony's boys. They'll pop me for sure." He bangs the butt of the gun against the faded clapboards and paint chips fly.

You try to say, "Help me." It comes out as a ragged whisper.

He walks back, gun hanging loose in his fist. "Sorry, pal." He pats your shoulder in sympathy. "You might not think so now, but I got worse troubles than you. I've got to lose myself, or I'm dead meat. But I'll call for help before I go."

He jams the gun in the waistband of his pants, gives a twisted smile. "So long, guy. Hope you pull through. I really mean it."

Wixom stuffs the crumpled summons in his jeans and runs back into the house. A few minutes later, he charges out the back door, cheap suitcase in one hand. "The paramedics are on the way. Hang on."

He disappears around the corner of the house. A minute later, the car starts up and screeches away.

Pull yourself into a sitting position and press your hanky to the wound. The slug has passed clean through at a shallow angle, giving you two new navels. Messy. Hurts like hell. Doesn't feel fatal.

Insurance will pick up the tab on the repair job.

Worker's Comp will pay for any time you're laid up.

Gleed and Crown will shell out for another suit to replace the one Wixom ruined.

You'll come out okay. But Wixom's slipped away again. Damn! Better run, jerk, fast and far!

You raise a red-stained middle finger toward taillights receding over a distant hill. The mob may give up on him after a while. But you won't. And the lawyers—Never!

For something to do before the medics arrive, something to take your mind off the fire in your side, fill in the form attached to your copy of Wixom's summons—he took the paper, didn't he? The crimson fingerprints are a nice touch. Don't forget to add Wixom's make of car and license plate number.

When you hear the wail of a siren approaching in the distance, put the paper away, tote up the day's earnings in your mind. Counting Wixom, about four hundred and fifty bucks.

All things considered, not a bad day. Not a bad day at all.

# LEAVING THE STATION

## MICHAEL DEL MURO

Victor sees the words Eat Our Shit tagged on the wall of the cement portion of the Los Angeles River. The words actually run together and are in all caps: EATOURSHIT. He sees these words while he travels on the commuter train past one of Los Angeles's many housing projects. There is a baseball field with dead, brown grass. The rims on the basketball courts are bent, and there are no nets. The only green Victor sees in the vicinity is the green water in the wash below the graffiti.

The trains that roll by every few minutes, twenty-four hours a day, undoubtedly shake the doors and windows and beds of those who live in the projects. The trains bring in people from wealthier neighborhoods, cities that a good portion of the people living in the projects will never see.

He was sure some kids from those projects wrote EATOURSHIT. Victor always tells nearby passengers that he'd be tempted to write EATOURSHIT if he lived in those projects and had to deal with the trains all day everyday.

While Victor is transfixed on the projects and the graffiti, the woman sitting next to him speaks up.

"There's some pretty nice cars there," she says, and Victor sees two white Mercedes-Benz SUVs. "Those are probably the drug dealers' cars."

Victor thinks of disagreeing with her out of principle. "No, cars and their televisions are the only comforts some of these people have," he wants to tell her. "When they work two jobs and are home only for sleep and an hour of leisure time, of course they would just want to travel in luxury and then veg out in front of a TV. Why do they have to be drug dealers?"

Instead, he says, "Probably."

With a whoosh, the train doors open.

This is when Victor is thankful for working in a city where the residents don't use public transportation. He often imagines how it'd be if he lived in cities like New York or Chicago. He wouldn't have a chance. The doors would slide open; the people would shove. A man the newspapers would call The Pusher would step behind him and shove him onto the tracks in front of an oncoming train. His body would get stuck between the train and the platform. Police would call his mother, and she would go and talk to him before they pulled the train away to let him die.

Instead, Victor steps off the train casually. There is a crowd, but not a big one. He walks, barely impeded, down a flight of stairs and then strolls across the station.

Sheriff deputies lead bomb-sniffing dogs, looking for the next unattended piece of baggage. People rush to one side of the station where they await their buses, but Victor walks the other way, out the front of the station and into downtown.

Victor walks down Main and sees Sam, a vagrant he had interviewed for a story about the city's huge homeless problem.

Sam doesn't recognize Victor; he suffers from a type of dementia.

"Change for food?" Sam asks.

"I have no cash," Victor says. The man surveys him, mumbles something, and then turns away. Victor feels guilty.

Victor thought that by becoming a reporter and writing about issues he cared about, he could actually make a difference. He doesn't believe that anymore.

For his story about Sam and the other homeless in the city, his newspaper received many letters of outcry from concerned citizens. But neither the city council nor the county board of supervisors took action. Victor didn't do anything either to help the homeless. He thought it'd be a violation of his reporter pledge to be completely independent, but as he walks away from Sam, he's not quite sure that that reasoning is accurate.

"Hey, Victor," Alice says as he enters the courthouse.

"My lady," he says as she traces the contours of his body with her metal-detecting wand. "Ooh, ooh. Just a little bit lower. Wow. I think I should at least buy you dinner after that."

She lets out a full-throated laugh that echoes in the hall and then says, "You know I'm married."

He and Alice have played that routine, or variations of it, hundreds of times since he started covering courts three years earlier.

He picks up his computer bag and walks toward a tiny office his paper keeps in the courthouse where reporters can file stories quickly to meet deadlines. The room contains nothing more than a small refrigerator, two desks, and Ethernet cords for Internet connection. A pretty woman, slightly younger than Victor, types away on her keyboard at the desk nearest a small three-foot-by-three-foot window about ten feet high on the cement wall.

"What do you have today?" Seema asks as Victor sits down at his desk.

"Guy killed his kids by lighting a barbeque in his house. Lone surviving daughter is testifying."

"That's probably why all the news vans are here," she says. "Good luck with that. I'm covering a double homicide. Wife walked in on her husband poking the neighbor's daughter. She poked them both with a butcher knife." She shrugs and goes back to her typing.

Victor settles into his seat and pulls his laptop out of his bag and starts typing.

"I have to go to my sister's school play tonight," she says after about twenty minutes of silence.

"Are you inviting me?"

"My parents will be there. You can finally meet them."

Victor pauses a few seconds.

"Can't I just go over to your place after the play?"

Her fingers continue to clatter along the keyboard, and she takes about five minutes before answering him.

"If that's what you want," she says finally.

Victor rereads the background information that he'll include in his article. He doesn't have to look at his notes to write the background either. He began covering this case the day of the tragedy. At the time, he was a beat reporter for a local newspaper. He arrived on the scene so early that day that he saw the paramedics pull out the five bodies and remembers the cops holding back the then fifteen-year-old daughter who had found them dead. He remembers her scream and how she cried and cried. He remembers the completely blank look in the girl's father's eyes as the police put him in the back of the patrol car.

He wrote stories about the murders almost every day for a month. He wrote about the fifteen-year-old girl, interviewing her classmates and teachers. He wrote about her dead brothers and sisters. He wrote about the father, the admitted perpetrator in the crime. He wrote about how the court-appointed attorneys planned to say that the man's wife's death led him to that temporary moment of insanity. His writing helped him land his current job at the city's major daily.

Victor is satisfied with what he writes and pulls out the day's paper. Death. War. Corruption. Same stories. Different people. He lowers the newspaper.

"Do you ever get tired of this crap?" he asks.

"No," Seema says without looking up from her monitor. "I like seeing my name in print."

As he often does when he's on a roll about some issue or another, Victor continues as if Seema hasn't said a word.

"I think I either need to quit, or I'm going to end up jumping off a building," he says.

"Don't do that," she says still not looking at him. "My parents haven't met you yet."

Victor takes the elevator and is surrounded by cops and lawyers.

He gets out and notices that most of those sitting on the benches and on the shiny floors in the hall that leads to the various courtrooms are either black or Hispanic. It's loud in the hall, despite the fact that most people whisper. Their combined whispers echo against the thick walls.

When he walks in the courtroom, the relative silence is in stark contrast to the noise outside. He takes his usual seat in the back of the courtroom and looks around. The children's grandparents on the mother's side are sitting close to him, and the star witness for the day, the surviving sister, now seventeen, sits between the two.

The girl's grandparents see him and smile those sad smiles of theirs, and he nods back. Then he sees the father's parents and nods to them.

He remembers how he cried after he wrote the story about their reaction to the murders and how their granddaughter didn't want to talk to them ever again. He was young then—twenty-seven or twenty-eight.

Victor raises his hand to acknowledge the bailiff, a deputy he's had lunch and drinks with several times.

Lisa, a reporter whose press pass identifies her from Channel 2, is sitting next to him with a notepad. Reporters from other newspapers and TV stations sit along his bench and the one in front of him.

"So give me the lowdown," she says.

Typical. She's attractive, and Victor guesses she's used to getting whatever she wants, including others to do the job for her.

"You haven't been following the case?" he asks, remembering that Channel 2 had a male reporter there a few days earlier.

"A bit," she says.

"Here," Victor says, handing her a folder filled with stack of stories he has written about the case. She starts flipping through the articles without saying a word. He carries them around to review even though he knows this case by heart. His coworkers call him a Boy Scout because he's always prepared.

An hour passes. Victor is used to this. Judges come into *their* courtroom at *their* leisure. He had always wondered what they did back in their offices. Were they like boxers who stalled in order to psych out their opponents? If that was the case, whom did they consider their opponents?

Finally, the door to the judge's chambers opens, and the bailiff calls, "All rise," and the trial is called to order.

The judge issues instructions. No tape recorders. No video recorders. Absolute silence. Harsh consequences.

When the prosecution calls its witness, Jennifer Velasquez, Victor begins to fiddle with his pen. It's actually one of those nifty recording pens that can secretly tape more than an hour's worth of audio. Although he's a reporter who follows journalistic ethics almost too rigidly, he explains the audio recorder simply as a way to make sure he doesn't use any inaccurate quotes.

"Raise your right hand," the bailiff commands. "Do you swear to tell the truth, the whole truth, and nothing but the truth, so help you God?"

"I do."

The courtroom seems to grow more silent as the girl lifts her eyes for the first time. She's beautiful. Victor hadn't seen her in more than a year, and she had changed.

He looks at the defendant, the girl's father, who has his head as low as it could possibly go. And not for the first time, he wonders why the man just didn't plead guilty.

"I know this is going to be tough for you," says Anna Martinez, the assistant district attorney in charge of the prosecution of the case. "But we need you to be strong for a few minutes."

The girl, already with tears in her eyes, nods and glances over at her father who has still not looked up. Anna touches the girl's hand.

"Where were you the morning the crimes took place?" she asks.

"At the beach with my friends."

"What time did you leave your house?"

"About ten thirty in the morning."

And the questioning goes on like this for about ten minutes.

Victor has seen Anna in action several times over the years. She's one of the toughest lawyers in the county, and although her rapid-fire questioning is her usual M.O., the gentleness in her voice today strikes him as peculiar. He jots down that detail debating whether it's something he could use in the article.

"Please, tell me what happened when you came home from the beach."

"Smoke was coming from the bottom of the front door," Jennifer says. "I thought it was a fire, so I called 911 before going into the house. I told them I thought there was a fire inside my house. They asked if anyone . . ." she pauses before continuing ". . . was inside. I said I wasn't sure."

She takes a few seconds to compose herself. Her father is crying, too. Victor writes this detail down in his notepad, as well.

The girl looks down to wipe the tears from her face. When she looks up, she stares straight at Victor. "My family dies," she tells him with her eyes, "and you sit in the back to see if you can get a good news story." Minutes seem to pass, and he has to look down.

Then she continues.

"I didn't want to wait. So I opened the door. The smoke smell was so strong. I shouted for my sister, but no one answered."

"Take your time," Anna says as Jennifer has begun to talk faster.

"Then I walked in"—she breathes in deeply and chokes up—"and saw Maribel on the kitchen floor. She was face down. Then I saw George next to her. He looked dead." She pauses. The judge hands her a tissue. She takes it and wipes her eyes. And once again, Victor notices her beauty. She's tall and dark, her hair is long and her lips are thick. She actually looks a lot like her father.

She looks at Victor again. "You're using us," he remembers her saying the last time he visited her grandparents.

Then in a fast, barely audible voice she says, "Then I saw Lucy, Mary, and Diego all in front of the TV. Their heads were down, and I didn't see them breathing."

Her chest heaves, and she sobs.

Anna walks over to Jennifer and holds her hand.

The judge whispers something to Jennifer, and she nods her head.

"Go ahead," he tells Anna.

"Where was your fath—I'm sorry . . . where was the defendant?"

Almost automatically, Jennifer glanced toward her father who still had his head lowered.

"He sat on the couch, saying 'I just needed it quiet' over and over."

"Are you going to take notes?" Lisa the TV reporter whispers to him.

Victor looks down at his notebook and realizes that he hasn't written anything down for a while, but he taps his recording pen.

"Smart move," Lisa whispers.

The prosecutor finishes questioning the girl. The defense attorney says that he does not have any questions for her.

The judge dismisses her and recesses until the next day.

"Where to?" Seema asks when Victor arrives back at their little office.

"Cathedral," Victor says.

The Cathedral of Our Lady of the Angels had become Victor and Seema's favorite lunch place. He hasn't gone to church in years, yet, on emotionally draining days, he finds comfort knowing that he is that close to one.

They walk the quarter mile from the courtroom to the cathedral.

"I want to go in today," he tells Seema after they order their food from the church's gourmet cafeteria.

"Why?"

"To pray," he thinks about saying.

"I don't know," he actually says. "I just want to go in. I'll be quick. Want to come with?"

She says something about the church burning down if she goes in and says she'll wait for their food. There is a mass, but Victor doesn't participate. Instead, he goes to the chapel downstairs, signs himself, kneels, but doesn't know what to do next. He hears the singing from the mass. Bells ring. He almost starts to cry.

Then he hears footsteps. He jumps up, embarrassed, and starts to walk back to the stairs. He walks so fast that he almost knocks down a young woman. Jennifer's face is dry now. At first, she looks surprised to see him, but a moment later, that surprise turns to suspicion, then to anger.

"Why are you here?" she asks.

"I wanted to—"

"Are you following me?"

Again, Victor notices her beauty. He wants to save her. He wants to take her and keep her for himself.

"Do I make a good story?" she asks. "What are you *doing* here?"

Before he responds, she lets her right hand fly, and the slap echoes throughout the chapel.

"I wanted to—" Victor starts again.

"What?" she yells. "You wanted to *what?*"

"I wanted to pray for you," he finally says.

Her face softens a bit, but before she can say anything, he runs upstairs and out of the cathedral. He doesn't care who sees him. He doesn't stop until he's inside the cafeteria.

"I can't write the story," he tells Seema when he sits down.

He sees the puzzled look on her face and continues. "I saw her."

"Who?"

"Jennifer Velasquez."

"*Who?*"

"The girl who just testified. The girl whose family was murdered by her own father."

Seema pauses for a few seconds, trying to process what Victor has just said.

"You'll get fired," Seema finally says. "You have to write it."

"I can't."

She looks at him for a few more seconds.

"You have to," she finally says. "Just write today's story and then ask off the case afterward."


Seema listens as Victor and his editor argue over the phone. Victor has told him that he'll pass along his notes to another reporter but can't, in his good conscience, write the story.

"We are using these people," he says.

Victor is silent while his editor talks.

Then Victor answers, "I know it's my job, but it's not right."

The editor talks some more.

"Okay," Victor says.

Seema doesn't wait for Victor to turn around and talk to her. "What did he say?" she asks.

"I write the story or I get fired."

"What are you going to do?"

Victor doesn't respond. He looks at his laptop. The cursor blinks, waiting for him to start typing. He looks at his notes. He thinks of all the stories he has written in the past. He thinks of the homeless in the streets that he has failed to help. He thinks of all the corrupt politicians he has interviewed and, in one way or another, has helped get elected. He thinks of all the tragedies he has exploited to further his career. He thinks of Jennifer and how the sooner the case gets out of the news the sooner she can continue her life. He looks at Seema. He looks at the screen. The cursor blinks.

What Victor likes most about covering courts is the hours. He starts earlier, but gets to go home at reasonable hours. His favorite days were those like this one with the testimony of a key witness being the sole purpose for him being at work.

He walks toward the exit and sees Alice.

"I'll be expecting that date when you and your husband call it kaput," he tells her.

"Sure thing, hon," she says, winking and then slapping Victor on the shoulder as he walks out. He turns around and gives her a hug. She's a little taken aback. He lets go and leaves.

It is ugly outside. Yellow. L.A. He walks toward the train station.

He sees the same homeless people he saw earlier in the day.

"Hey, can you spare some change for some food?" says one homeless man he often sees while walking.

"I don't have any change," Victor says. But he hands him some food that he had leftover from lunch. The man thanks him and Victor continues to walk. He walks toward Olvera Street and orders some tacos and a beer at his favorite restaurant in the city. He takes his time drinking the beer. He will catch the seven p.m. train. He orders another beer. And another. Finally, when he feels a little tipsy, but not drunk—he'll be meeting Seema's parents later and wants to make a good impression—he walks toward a small truck that sells churros and buys four. He eats them one by one, enjoying every bite until he starts to feel ill. Then he walks across the street into Union Station. His train waits for him. He boards and falls asleep. He wakes up when the train begins to roll. He pulls a piece of paper out of his pocket and looks at it. He's never been more proud of something he has written.

The train rolls out and heads toward home.

He sees the graffiti: EATOURSHIT.

"Not anymore," he whispers to himself. "Not anymore."

# GONE ACCOURTING

## LIZ HUFFORD

## THE SUMMONS

No herald announces its arrival, sandwiched between fliers for services I will never use and bills I must pay. I have been summoned. Summoned is an archaic, if appropriate, term. It conveys an air of importance as in, "Milady, the queen has summoned you to the castle." Exciting yes, but there is an element of danger; Death also summons. Holding the paper before me, I remark like *Everyman* to Death, "You came when I least expected you." My "death," of course, is symbolic, like that of a medieval anchorite. In Arizona, I must serve one day or one trial. At that time, I am sequestered, cut off from the world except for the occasional cell phone recess.

It is not my first call to duty. Over the years, the tone of the summons has become sterner. I wonder how many jurors simply fail to appear. Assuming citizenship, only the presiding judge can dismiss a prospective juror. A friend tried to get his wife, an Alzheimer's patient, excused from service with a letter from her doctor. His request was refused. At considerable inconvenience, he delivered her to court, babbling and incoherent. The judge thanked them for their trouble and sent them home. Able and willing jurors may be endangered species.

The summons's date coincides with the last final exam I will give this semester so I follow the directions for a one-time deferral of service. A few days later, a second summons arrives, confirming my selected date.

## THE LOTTERY

Once service is performed, a citizen cannot be called for additional jury duty for eighteen months. Every eighteen months a summons arrives for me. Why is this? I live in a county of nearly four million. Why can't I be this lucky in the state lottery?

Griping about jury duty is guaranteed by the constitution. It is one of the few things all parties agree on. If I complain to friends, they share secrets for avoiding jury duty. Don't vote. Don't pay taxes. These alternatives don't work for me, and I begin to suspect that is why I am called, not summoned this time, but called.

But Faustus-like, I still hope to escape my fate. I am to phone after four o'clock the day before my required service; the case may settle out of court. I listen intently to the recording. Several jury groups must report at eight a.m.—not mine. A few more are due at ten— not mine. I begin to feel lucky. Then the recording intones that I must telephone at eleven on my day of service. Monday, I make the call. I have less than two hours to appear at the courthouse.

## OF MY PEERS

A day-pass for the city's new light rail system was enclosed with my summons.

The court is downtown in a warren of one-way streets, deferred construction, and few parking places. I rode the light rail free the weekend it opened. I decide to use my pass as an opportunity to nail down the system.

I drive to the northern-most stop of the light rail and park. I figure out which of the many slots my day-pass goes in and stamp it. I am now riding legally, unlike an estimated third of the passengers. Aboard the train, something occurs to me. A defendant is entitled to a jury of his peers. What is a jury of peers?

Sometimes I feel as if I live in a sociological bubble. I reside in a gated community. I drive to work every day in the solitude of my car. My campus, though devoid of ivy and towers, is an educational microcosm. When I am there, among students and teachers, I am with my peers.

But the law's definition of peers is broader. Who are my peers in terms of the law? I bet they ride the light rail.

The train is new, clean, and quiet. My peers not so much. Across from me sits an older Native American woman. Her frosted hair and pink shorts are not traditional. She picks invisible lint from her black purse, talking, singing, or chewing the whole time. There is little noise, but her mouth and fingers move continually from boarding to departure. The doors open, and a man sits next to me. He is odiferous but not offensive. He smells, not of B.O. or liquor, but like history—wood smoke, leaf mold, and horses. At the next stop, a gaggle of black girls board. Their banter fills the car. Two of the young women are beauties, Taylor, her decorated notebook provides her name, and Washeena. A young black businessman sits across from them. He wears Dolce & Gabbana sunglasses and sports a square, four-faced wristwatch framed in diamonds. He communes with his iPhone. I hear the girls as white noise. I am not following their conversation until the black man speaks.

"You girls on your way to school?"

They nod.

"Do they teach you words there?"

The girls look at one another.

"Why don't you use those words rather than cuss words?"

The girlish banter becomes a low rumble. Then Taylor asserts, "I'm moving. I don't have to put up with disrespectful shit." The girls crowd the door. The black man shakes his head and looks at me. "They should have their asses whipped." The girls raise eyebrows and mock his language. As he leaves the car, they boo and heckle. They depart en masse at the next stop.

Now I am alone with a young man with close-cropped hair and a neatly trimmed beard and moustache. He sports tattoo cuffs from wrist to elbow, an eclectic mixture of peace signs, Celtic symbols, and fists. Large letters are tattooed around his neck. For a long while, I can see only "acker"—I strum through the alphabet. Is he a backer? hacker? whacker? The images are very different. Finally, he twists his neck for a view, and I see he is a cracker. Of course.

A young woman sits next to me and chats. She recently moved to Arizona and landed her dream job. She says hello to everyone who boards. "My co-workers say I shouldn't talk to everyone—that it will get me killed, but, hey, I'm a West Virginia girl."

I reach my stop and say goodbye; I'm a Pennsylvania, small-town girl myself.

## THE ASSEMBLY LINE

This is a bureaucracy that works. Minutes after my arrival, my name is called along with thirty-something others. Our trial is scheduled for the bonus courtroom, which entails a trek of several blocks. It is one hundred and three degrees, and our long line of lemmings follows the bailiff through the melting streets. Because we are with the bailiff, we get a pass on security clearance. Does he already know our faces or is he relying on numbers? If there were one too many of us, would we all have to be rescreened? Recently, an accused child molester on trial managed to walk out of the courthouse wearing a judge's robe.

We file into the courtroom in numerical order. The judge, a woman, gives instructions. We are numbers here. We must answer yes or no; shakes and nods and uhuhs make the court recorder's task harder. The case is aggravated DUI, the defendant had no license when the offense occurred.

We introduce our nameless selves, holding our number in front of us and responding to the questions on the back. Easy stuff—our occupation, marital status, children. Jury selection involves answering a series of questions. The whole group is asked if the defendant does not appear, would that sway our opinion? The judge tells us this cannot be a factor in deliberations. She asks if service would cause undue hardship. The self-employed raise hands and sweat loss of income—hairdressers, lawn men, and consultants. The caregivers chime in, forced to leave new babies or ailing seniors. Then the judge asks if any of us, or a close family member, has been convicted of DUI. Hands go up. Details are gleaned in numerical order. Things get personal.

## THE JERRY SPRINGER SHOW

The judge has clearly stated that jurors may make their explanations in private, that is without the other jurors present. But few people avail themselves of that opportunity. They may all be desperate to avoid service and anxious to leave as quickly as possible. Or maybe jury rooms are like airplanes. You'll never see the passenger seated next to you again, so why not bare all?

Thirty-some people in the room and a whole world of hurt. One child killed by a drunk driver. A father murdered. Two male senior citizens still brutalized by memories of alcoholic fathers.

I find myself hoping that this is creative fiction, that my peers are spinning fantastic stories to avoid their duty. If so, these prospective jurors have more talent than my average creative writing class.

I seldom need to elaborate on my answers. I am not a member or regular donor to MADD. I am not a teetotaler. When asked if I have relatives in law enforcement, I reply that an uncle was a chief of police and a cousin an officer. The judge asks if they were employed in Arizona.

"Florida and Pennsylvania," I reply.

I seem removed from these peers. The last time I was summoned, the case involved child porn. "If you were molested as a child, please raise your hand."

When it was my turn, the judge asked. "Would that experience impinge upon your ability to render an impartial verdict in this case?"

"No, your honor."

I was not selected.

Jury selection takes hours. One juror answers in the affirmative to every question, and her follow-up explanations are elaborate. We learn her philosophy of life and don't care. We know she will not be selected but not because of bias. Jurors may ask questions during the trial; this woman could make a three-day trial last a week or more.

We wish she would shut up.

The court recesses so the prosecution and the defense can select the jury. We mill just outside the courtroom, texting, reading, using the facilities. Occasionally, one of us is called in for a follow-up question. Finally, we are all called to order. Nine people will be chosen, a jury with one alternate. Once again we play the lottery. My number, thirty-four, is called in the ninth position. All the others are excused—the caregivers, the self-employed, and the alcohol-damaged. I shrug and take my place to be sworn. Who better to serve than I?

## THE TRIBE

In the great gathering room, hundreds of people paid little attention to each other, but now we are reduced to nine, a fraternity of strangers. Our manners improve, and we make small talk. We are financial advisors, mechanics, teachers, and the unemployed. The thing we can't discuss is the only thing we have in common. The judge tells us we will hear the case beginning tomorrow and finish it on Wednesday. She reminds us not to discuss the case with friends and family, and we are in recess.

## THE CASE

The prosecutor, a large, young woman, is very thorough presenting her case. The defendant drove a car, which had already lost a wheel, off the highway and into a gate. Then he backed up the vehicle and crashed into the gate again. She has the surveillance videos from the incident and a tape of his booking interview in a mobile DUI unit.

He appears to be a very likable, drunken man. Two lawmen, the gatekeeper, the record manager of the DMV, and a forensic scientist testify. The defendant was sent five different notices that his license had been suspended. The breathalyzer was accurate. The prosecutor is building a brick house; we wait to see if the defense can blow it down.

The defense attorney accepts most of the expert testimony stressing that there were two other men with names similar to the defendant's. At one time during his interview, the defendant said his brother was driving, but no one else is visible in the surveillance video. Still, the defense's approach is that this is a case of mistaken identity.

We begin to realize why the defendant may not appear in court. If he did, and he was the same guy as the taped interview, there would be no defense. By now, we are pretty sure that the defense is a public defender with very little to work worth. The prosecutor, on the other hand, may be new to her job. She seems to have covered every aspect of the case but still is not sure she has done enough. She begins to remind me of the talkative prospective juror.

After the prosecution finishes, we wait for the defense to pull together all the small questions he raised regarding identity into a reasonable defense. Instead he rests. The judge checks her watch and tells us to return in the morning for closing arguments.

## NINE MEN ON THE FIELD

We are nine, but one of us is an alternate to be selected at random. On this last day, we realize it is important to us to know how the trial turned out. The financial advisor and I exchange emails. If one of us is the alternate, the other will email the verdict. It occurs to me that literature may be a search for justice. Not every story must provide it. Indeed if they did, there would be little need for a search. But is it the central metaphor of all story? Of what we wish from life?

As we assemble in the jury room, one of us is missing—the oldest juror. She needed to be driven to the bonus courtroom that first day, and she chided a juror who began to talk about the plaintiff's interview during one of our recesses. She simply doesn't show, so no drawing of names is necessary. We, the jury, are about to play Solomon.

## BEHIND CLOSED DOORS

After the prosecutor reiterates her case and the defense repeats what little he has, we are sequestered. One man keeps asking why the defendant did not appear? We remind him that that is not a consideration in reaching our decision, but, of course, it is, given the stolen identity defense. All the evidence points to a guilty verdict, and there is no conflict among us. This part never fails to amaze me. These jurors, my peers, for all our differences, respond to the rule of reason. We report back to court with the verdict.

"Now can we ask questions about the case?" one juror asks.

The judge nods.

"Why didn't the defendant appear?"

"We can't find him," the judge says.

We have convicted a fugitive. If he should ever try to cross the border back into the U.S., he'll be nabbed.

## SO LONG, FAREWELL

We say our goodbyes; they are not prolonged. As pragmatically as we came together, we split apart. I'm back on the light rail, among my peers. It's a different crew—a woman with vodka in her water bottle, an artist with a wrapped canvas under his arm, a cyclist. As a teacher, I am well aware of the intellectual differences between students. A class may contain a genius, the dullest tool in the shed, and the full spectrum in between. Is my class half empty or half full? What happened today happens every time I have jury duty. I marvel at the wisdom of our forefathers. A jury, a single entity of disparate parts, responds to the rule of reason, and each individual has a role to play.

retainers

attorneys know there is no profit
in toiling for the wind
they deal in hard facts
retainers in hand before they
sit and roll and speak
for their masters

they know the foolishness
of expending energy on possibilities
the future is irrelevant to them
concepts of rewards on a higher plane
have no place in their lives
they leave such philosophies
to judges and their masters

—*Joseph A. Farina*

## criminal courtroom

these walls reverberate
with hungry voices
competing for my soul
some whisper desperation
prophesying my defeat
some whisper abandonment
urging me to walk away
into their safe oblivion
still listening
for the one clear voice
that will not lie
i stand, contemplating choices
and the intentions of my heart

—*Joseph A. Farina*

## principles of sentencing
## (juvenile court)

robed in black with a blood red sash
he weighs the evidence presented
sifting out the lies, ignoring what he must
to convict the boy before him, legally adult—
now crying for his mother
who holds him in unquestioned love
her eyes upon the judge—imploring—
for a sentence from a father
beneath official robes

—*Joseph A. Farina*

transubstantiation

they pour out their grievances
in blood and grief, anger and fear
upon my desk
where i gather and transform them
into black and white
a sum total of their journey
of love, lies, and betrayal
onto cold legal-sized paper
bound by paper clips and staples
measuring out their lives

—*Joseph A. Farina*

# AFFIRMED

ANTHONY J. MOHR

Everyone rose on the bailiff's command. Judge Janice Calley swept into her courtroom, paused to let the bailiff announce that court was in session, and ascended to her bench. No one sat until the judge had settled into her leather chair and made a downward hand gesture to the audience. As attorneys moved toward the counsel table, Judge Calley noted with satisfaction that her staff had arranged things well. The briefs were neatly placed in front of her with key passages tabbed. Two pens and two pencils lay in a grooved area constructed to hold them. To her right was a pad of legal paper with "Superior Court" printed at the top, and next to the pad was a cup, not a mug, for her tea.

She listened to six lawyers beg her to continue a trial because they were settling. Their only remaining task involved selling some unspecified "product" that was on consignment. Judge Calley noted that the men pressed their palms together in a classic suppliant gesture every time they uttered the word "product." She glanced at the clock on the wall, just in time to see the minute hand jerk forward. "Counsel, I've heard enough. If you want to settle your case, do so by the trial date. Your request for a continuance is denied. Next case: Porter versus Powertrain, Inc."

Ten minutes later, Judge Janice Calley signed a temporary restraining order freezing Powertrain's assets and barring the company from doing any more business in California. "The hearing on the preliminary injunction will be July twentieth. I want the CEO here for live testimony."

Fighting to maintain his composure, Powertrain's lawyer said, "Your Honor, my client has prepaid vacation plans that week." There it is again, the judge thought to herself. The supplicant position, palms pushed together, hands raised in prayer mode. She had lost count of how many had beseeched her with such body language.

"You mean your client *had* vacation plans," Her Honor calmly replied. "The record shows your client has dodged too many of his commitments over the past year. You and he are out of excuses. I am ordering your client to be here on July twentieth." She had to admit she felt righteous, as well as powerful.

"Your Honor, I am supposed to be in arbitration that day," the lawyer began, but she cut him off.

"That will have to wait, I'm afraid. Give my clerk the arbitrator's phone number, and we'll let him know he has to adjourn it. Court's in recess." She whacked her gavel one minute before four thirty, a fitting end for a Friday afternoon.

The judicial secretary took advantage of Judge Calley's passage from bench to chambers to hand her a telephone message slip. Calley took it with a nod and stuffed the paper in her pocket. The court attendant held the chambers door while the judge strode in with her clerk and research attorney hurrying behind. "If you please, Judge," asked her clerk, "what do you want to do with the hearing in Kerr versus Dinnerman? You set the Powertrain hearing at the same time."

"Move Kerr."

"The attorneys are coming from out of state."

"Powertrain's more important." She dropped into her chair

without removing her robe. "Okay, Andrew, we have work to do on the oil refinery motions. You need to research these three issues before next Friday's hearing." Andrew wrote furiously, and he thanked her when she finished. Calley noticed that Andrew always ended their conversations by thanking her, a soldier's reflex.

Even though she was not cold, the judge kept her robe on while she sat at her work table and reread the nine motions that were on Monday's calendar. Comfortable with her intended rulings, she looked ahead to the Tuesday pile. It contained only two motions, both routine, because a trial was scheduled to begin. Again, she knew how she'd rule.

The judge hung her robe in the closet and paused to look at it. In gold thread, her initials, JC, were stitched into the material where they would touch the back of her neck. She ran a hand across the black fabric and smiled.

Judge Calley started for the door, then stopped and returned to her desk. She wanted to reread a California Supreme Court opinion that had come down today, affirming one of Judge Calley's most difficult rulings. In their unanimous opinion, the seven justices had gone out of their way to praise her management of what they termed "an extraordinarily difficult case that presented many complex legal questions." Halfway through the decision, Judge Calley's grin faded when she realized that it was time to leave. The Judicial Security Unit worried about judges remaining alone in the courthouse after dark. Janice Calley printed another copy to take home and savor once she got under the covers.

The judges' elevator offered a particularly pleasant enclosure, for overlaying its walls was a soft material, and the floor was parquetry. Riding it up to her rarefied job was one of those small experiences to which the judge looked forward every Sunday night. But this was Friday night. When the doors opened at the judges' parking level, she fingered the phone message in her pocket and felt a stab of tension.

The freeway traffic was light. The western edge of the L.A. sky was still red with sunset. The weekend lay ahead, open and free. Judge Calley blinked her eyes and gripped the wheel slightly harder. Her cell phone lay on the passenger seat, but she did not know whom to call. She was moving too quickly for a Friday night. Where the hell is the traffic, she asked herself. Everyone must have left early for the weekend. Janice Calley wondered where and with whom, then chided herself for not taking surface streets. They would have been slower tonight and besides, Judicial Security encouraged her to vary her commuting route. She was going to arrive home too soon.

Janice Calley exhaled when she reached the turnoff to her neighborhood, knowing that within ten minutes she would walk across the Persian rug in her foyer and turn right into the living room, no, better to turn left into the dining room and from there to the kitchen and place her briefcase on the table in the breakfast nook. But she had no briefcase because she had completed her work for Monday. She could go to the kitchen and make a snack, as long as it was not fattening. Then she could read or rent a movie.

As Judge Janice Calley pondered her choices, her fingers obediently moved to the telephone and started tapping integers. She stared at the message slip, penned in her secretary's neat handwriting: "Your father."

Fernando was answering the phones this evening. "Oh, Honorable Judge!" he exclaimed in his Tagalog accent, as he always did when she called. He put Janice through to her father.

"I miss your mother," he said.

"I do, too, Daddy."

"How long's it been?"

Janice said, "Six years."

"I need you at the store." His voice sounded firm.

"Daddy, Jake is running the store just fine."

"He doesn't . . . talk enough with the customers. Doesn't build loyalty. You need that in the grocery business."

"The sales are up," she answered, in a tone that sounded like a request instead of a statement.

"That doesn't matter. More people live around there now. They'll build more supermarkets."

"They already have. Jake's got a good nitch—"

"Don't debate me. I gotta go over there. Can you drive me?"

Janice gripped the receiver. "Daddy I have a bar association reception tonight, and they're expecting me to—"

Frank Calley interrupted his daughter. "The store's a valuable family asset. You got to get more involved in it."

Janice began to sweat. She knew what would come next and regretted telling her father that Superior Court judges got thirty vacation days a year. She had been on the bench two weeks, savoring a delicious new world of respect and power and had gushed about the job benefits to her parents over dinner one night. Now, seven years after that meal, vacation time constituted the one factoid Frank Calley remembered about his daughter's job.

What she said had been tried before. "Daddy, I am involved in the store. Jake keeps me informed, and I give him suggestions."

"No, you've gotta take some of your unlimited vacation time and help out."

She attempted a subject change. "The house looks really good, Daddy. I just had it painted. Mommy would approve."

He cleared his throat. "We liked living there. But I get three meals a day here. So what are you doing tomorrow morning?" Janice was planning to sleep, or read in bed, or go for a run before meeting Barbara and Vicky for brunch. She knew what he'd say. Homework was the only excuse forty years ago, and work was the only excuse today. She paused too long in search of an answer to his question, and into the silence, her father said, "Come by at eight, and we'll go with Jake to the store."

Janice conceded with a mild "all right." Then her voice speeded up. "Daddy, one other thing. The Supreme Court unanimously affirmed me today, and they published the opinion. It was a big case and they upheld me on every point—"

She heard a voice from the intercom in her father's room, garbled except for the word 'dinner.' "I'm hungry, Janice," her father said. "I'll see you tomorr—" Each word sounded softer as Frank Calley's receiver moved toward its cradle.

The morning sun streamed through a skylight and illuminated the photos of Janice's family that hung in her hall. While her other relatives were pictured together at a picnic, a hearth, or a park, someone had snapped Janice's father alone in his grocery store, head tilted back, counting the inventory on the top shelves, smiling while he performed the hard work that, he insisted, honored and ennobled the human race. Janice shook her head and moved on to the kitchen. She skimmed the California section of the *Times* as she ate a banana and dipped her croissant through the white froth and deep into the cappuccino.

Frank Calley said nothing during the five minutes it took Janice and her brother to help him across the porte-cochere and into Jake's SUV. Not until they got within a mile of the store did he speak: "Jake, what were the receipts last month?" Jake told him, a number sufficient to make Frank nod his head.

"Are you planning any specials for Columbus Day?"

"I might. That's two months away. The Labor Day program didn't do much for us."

Jake's father coughed and cleared his throat. "You have Italians in the neighborhood, and there's more profit in pasta and sausages than hamburgers and chips. Plan for Columbus Day."

"I'll work on it, Father," Jake said.

"Janice, you need to help your brother plan something special—"

"Daddy," Janice cut in quickly, but Jake stopped both of them, for they had reached the store and he wanted to introduce them to Michael, the new assistant.

"Where's Wayne?"

"I told you last week, he moved away, to the Rockies."

"You hired this new man without—without—an interview with me?"

"Father, you just got out of the hospital, and I needed someone. And he's good, and I didn't want to lose him. You're going to meet Michael now. You'll like him."

Despite ten years in California, Michael retained a slight Bronx accent. On his right forearm was a colored tattoo of a mermaid, something Janice saw before noticing his thick black hair. As Michael led them to the stockroom, Janice realized that he moved like a cat, but he was a polite cat. He waited for Janice's father to shamble down the aisle before explaining how he and Jake had rearranged the shelves to accommodate more inventory. The cans of marinara sauce were still on shelf number five, but the long boxes of vermicelli had been moved to eye-level. Also new was the computer. Recently installed software allowed them to track customer buying patterns. Janice smelled the fresh paint that made the stockroom actually pleasant, not the musty place she remembered from her youth. She watched Jake smile when Michael neared the end of his presentation. After Michael finished, Janice nodded her head at the same time that she saw her father's jaw start working.

"How many of your customers do you know by name?"

Michael answered quickly. "Probably twenty. Give me time, Mr. Calley. I'll learn them."

"You spend your time with computers and—and making it nice in the back room. You need to be out front." Frank Calley looked at his son, not at Michael.

"Father, we had to fix things back there. We didn't know where half the merchandise was."

"Aaah, I need to spend time here with you. You're not ready yet, Jake. And Janice, you need to come down here more often and—"

Jake interrupted, "Dad, can we talk about this in private?"

"I'm tired," his father said.

While Michael serviced two customers, Jake made sandwiches, tuna fish for Janice, roast beef for his father, and turkey pastrami for himself. He added a generous dollop of coleslaw and two pickles before wrapping the meals in butcher paper and stuffing them into a bag along with a large container of fruit salad and cans of Sprite, Diet Coke, and root beer. A manila envelope lay near the cash register, and Jake took it along with the bag that held their lunch. Janice escorted her father to the SUV while Jake and Michael talked alone for a few moments. She helped him in, adjusted his sport coat, and reached across to fasten his shoulder harness. Frank Calley made a frustrated noise as he tried unsuccessfully to grasp the seat belt, for his left arm would not obey.

Jake tuned the radio to the Broadway Channel during the ride. Frank Calley kept his eyes closed and let his head sway gently to the music. His lips stretched into a dreamy grin, and Janice could swear that his wrinkles were fading. When they reached the home, Sky and Sarah were in the middle of "If I Were a Bell." No one left the car until several seconds after the song had ended and Frank Calley's eyes slid open.

His eyes started closing again after he ate his sandwich. "You want us to put your fruit salad in the refrigerator for later?" Janice asked. "And I didn't eat my sandwich." Frank Calley nodded at his daughter. He shuffled toward the elevator, more slowly than usual, Janice thought, and when he arrived there, he hugged Jake before touching the call button. Janice noted that Jake was now over a head taller than his father. Frank's hands, darkened from IVs, trembled gently as they gripped Jake's shoulders. "Jake, I'm proud of you. You're doing a good job at the store."

"Thanks, Father," Jake answered in a sweet voice. "You taught me a lot. I'll make it work." He was looking over his father's shoulder, at an attractive woman who was pushing a man in a wheelchair.

"Janice, promise me you'll spend time at the store."

"I promise, Daddy." Janice was amazed at the sincerity in her voice.

"I want you and Jake to have something to work on together. To keep you close and keep—keep—you," Frank Calley paused a beat, and then continued. "You've gone far in life. Help out at the store. It reminds you where we came from."

"I won't ever forget, Daddy," Janice promised. She kissed him on the cheek. His skin felt rough; he smelled antiseptic.

"Jake, call me tomorrow. I want to talk to you about Columbus Day."

"Will do, Father."

Jake and Janice returned to the table in the patio, where he finished his fruit cup and root beer. "I called Barbara and Vicky and moved my lunch back an hour," she said.

"This won't take long," Jake said. He opened the manila envelope. "Just sign where they put the stickers."

"I guess I ought to read this first?" Janice asked lightly. "It's the lingering attorney in me."

"Your former law partner did an excellent job," Jake said. The document was blue-backed, precise in type and margin. As she was taught to do in practice, Janice initialed each page of the agreement of purchase and sale.

"What are you going to do with your share?" Jake asked as he handed her a check. "Mine's already spent, of course. Amber and Josh's college fund."

"I wish I knew. Ask me next week."

Outside in the parking lot, Janice and her brother looked up involuntarily at the second story window, the fourth from the left. Its curtain was drawn. Their father would call them later to say how refreshed he felt after sleeping three hours.

"I like Michael," Janice said.

"He's not your type." Jake chuckled.

"I know. But I like him. Is he trustworthy?"

"You saw him today. Did he act like a perfect underling or what?"

Janice nodded in agreement. After a moment, she asked, "Does he think he can turn the store around?"

"He says he can. I hope so. We'll get a kicker if he succeeds. And anyway, it gives us some semblance of a reason to take Father there occasionally."

"You think Daddy will ever find—"

Jake cut her off. "Who's going to tell him?"

Judge Calley gave Barbara and Vicky a tour of her courtroom after their lunch, and she lingered in chambers once they left. It would start turning dark soon, time to think about what she wanted to do between now and bedtime. Maybe stop at the supermarket to get herself some chicken and rent a movie. She turned on her computer. An email notification glowed on the screen. The Chief Judge of the Superior Court had written it at nine a.m. Judge Calley read the message quickly at first; then, after closing her eyes for a moment, with care. She printed two copies, one for chambers, the other to take home. Judge Janice Calley's eyes blinked as she savored the Chief's words, now firmly in her hand, as well as her head: "Just saw what the Supreme Court had to say about you. What a wonderful job, Janice. You're a terrific colleague. I'm so proud of you."

## May it Please the Court

*Oyez, oyez, oyez,*
chants the court crier.
All rise as seven judges
robed in black file in
to the majestic chamber.
Row upon row
of appellate advocates
wait their turn.

She's turned out
in a black suit
with a forties flair—
a nod to Lauren Bacall.
Dressed in black patent
pumps, sheer black hose,
an extra pair stuffed
in her briefcase.
Just enough gold to glint.

Facts honed with a lathe.
Legal principles loaded
like a spring gun.
Only fifteen minutes
to present her client's case.
Years of anger and anguish
summarized in Times Roman
font on recycled white paper,
bound by Rules of Court.

Seven judges robed in black
pound her with questions.
She dodges, deflects, then
swings with white gloves.
The red light blinks.

*Your time is up counselor.*

Months later: edict issued, precedent set.
Plaintiff and defendant pressed
into law books like dried flowers.

—*Leslie B. Neustadt*

# AMICUS, BRIEFLY

JULIET HUBBELL

He was a judge, and he was a good one—fair and thoughtful and above all, knowledgeable concerning the law and its various statutes. But he had a habit of leaning back in his chair, closing his eyes, and rubbing his very thick, dark eyebrows that was off-putting to the many defendants brought before him. Perhaps it was this pained air, this seeming discomfort at having to bear up under the halting and inept excuses of such unfortunate persons that kept him from ever gaining a higher level of judgeship than the county courts.

He had aspired to much grander things, the appellate courts, certainly, and if he were the divulging sort of man, he would even have admitted to imagining a life at the state Supreme Court level. But he was not that sort of man. He had a wife, one son. They were so much a part of his daily life, had always been, that he hardly considered them separate from himself. They consulted one another often during the course of a week in regard to all the events and activities that three related individuals might share. Yet, he did not divulge much. Not even to them.

He put on the dark navy robe over his smooth, finely tailored suit each morning and never got over feeling slightly foppish in it. His suits were exquisite; he could instantly recognize tight, flat weaves from Italy or the silky, intricate weave of material from Asia. He could just as easily have worn khaki slacks and a cheap cotton shirt under the gown, for it hid everything save his tie. But he seemed to realize that others would know, that what he wore underneath would somehow betray him.

He spent many hours during the week maintaining his physique, however, and the ample robe often left him feeling disappointed, as if he had dressed up for nothing. The sleeves flowed, and sometimes he found himself tangled in the extra fabric as he reached for the gavel to punctuate the conclusion of a hearing or a settlement. He often eyed the court reporter, a woman he had come to know well over the years and whom he thoroughly distrusted. She never looked at the keys in front of her and instead greatly enjoyed the activity of the courtroom that milled and churned all about her, including watching him become, however briefly, ensnarled in his sleeves.

The bailiff was a friend of his, a man whom, by contrast, he innately trusted. He wore a gun as easily as a man wears a pair of favorite briefs; it had become an easy, comfortable accessory. If a defendant became agitated or even bellicose after the judge had pronounced the court's finding, he could see out of the corner of his eye that the bailiff had already risen from his seat and had his hands resting lightly, one on his hip, the other on the holster. Sometimes the bailiff even moved in between the judge and an angry defendant, a gesture the judge found endearing.

At the end of the day, he would retire to the room behind the courtroom. He would enter the key code and then push the heavy, walnut door, listening to its thick, solid click as it shut and locked automatically. Sometimes he would pause just at the doorway, feeling the door shut, enjoying the close, quiet embrace of his own office. The windows looked down three floors onto the county court's plaza and stairs, and farther off, he could see the dark, concrete parking structure. He never shut the ornately brocaded draperies. He would open the windows often, hoping for a breeze or perhaps to catch snatches of conversation floating up from the plaza. Yet, even in the fall, when the Santa Ana winds would blow with a parching, fiercely hot persistence, the judge's chamber never seemed to usher them in.

He often stood for long periods of time, reflecting on the day's parade of ill-destined citizens. He would gaze down at the groups of people, attorneys with briefcases dangling from their hands, street toughs smoking and talking animatedly with mothers or sullen girlfriends. He would place a hand on his chest as if feeling heart palpitations, but his breath would become deep and regular as if he were meditating. When the sun had finally begun to set, he would watch the people trickle away into the deepening shadows, into cars and buses. He would give a long exhalation and lift the polished silk of his tie into his fingers, suspend it in air for a moment, and let it drop noiselessly back to his chest. Last, he would turn away from the sight, head bowed, and walk, like a man convicted, to his desk.

## Reading the PSI

He tells himself it is not about him.
It is about each of them on the docket,
the ragged parade of broken narratives,
soldiers at war with their dwindling better parts,
surrendered to metastatic grief.

Pre-Sentence Investigation Report:
At age six, mother dead of overdose.
Father murdered same year.
Foster mother and her daughter
forced defendant to perform oral sex on them.
Ran away at thirteen. Crack ever since
(except when incarcerated). Cannot recall
if he had siblings (though an earlier PSI reports
he was sixth of eight). Fathered no children, he says
(though the prior PSI names his daughter, Tamieka).
He states his life is unmanageable; he is misunderstood.

Not about him, yet the judge is defined by them,
the sense of open wounds, the sense of falling,
the rough edges of agonal respiration,
certain that pain is proof of breathing.
Made of doubt, reasonable doubt
in the fissures where evidence was
but fled or was taken for a price.
He tries to smile.

These men and women are his reason
to listen, to attend with great care
the vague, disproven hopes, predicting
the thrumming threat of storms, gatherings
of shapeless smoke before the funnel.
Helpless, he is watchful for moments,
rarest of incandescent moments.

—*Charles Reynard*

# HUNTZ'S LAW

TOM GREEN

Judge Andrew Huntz graduated thirty-fifth out of one hundred in his law school class. It wasn't as high as he'd wanted, but perhaps it was higher than he deserved. He'd discovered alcohol in law school, specifically scotch. It wasn't the single malt stuff he drank now—and were he to encounter a glassful of the rotgut he drank back then, he'd dispose of it promptly and deny that he'd ever even heard of the stuff—but at the time it had been a revelation. He drank to take the edge off his torts classes. He drank to get in the right mood to study. He drank to shake off the deeply ingrained shyness that had kept him a virgin far longer than he'd ever admitted to anyone. He drank for the sake of drinking, and if that had knocked him ten or so places down in his class, he thought he'd more than made up for it with all the networking he'd learned to do with a drink in his hands. In fact, were he to really think about it, Judge Andrew Huntz might have given much of the credit for his present station to his favorite beverage.

Judge Huntz may have graduated thirty-fifth in his class, but of the thirty-four men in front of him, only six others were judges. Sure, many of the sixty-five behind him were judges, too, a couple of them federal, but Judge Huntz didn't care about them because he'd proven his superiority back in law school. It was the thirty-four in front of him that Judge Huntz focused on, and despite his courthouse and his bench and all his authority gathered here in the fifth circuit, he felt there was still something missing.

"I need to get on television," he said one September afternoon as he sat in his chambers, sipping a single malt and fondling a cigar that he was not allowed to smoke indoors thanks to some legislation with which he personally disagreed. He'd been assured by most everyone who worked in his courthouse that no one would say a word if he felt the need to light up every now and again, but he'd always refused. Judge Huntz believed the law, no matter how stupid it may have been at times, applied to everyone. Even to judges who enjoyed a smoke with their scotch more than almost anything in the world.

"Yes, that's what I need. A case that gets me on television," he said, as if there had been some momentary debate over his initial pronouncement.

Lionel Baker, who'd been Judge Huntz's clerk for three years now, was sorting through the judge's mail at a table on the other side of the room. In truth, the judge had forgotten Lionel was even there, and so he was surprised to hear a response to his musings.

"Television? Are you sure about that, Your Honor?" Lionel asked.

The judge whipped his head around, no easy feat since his neck was embedded in a thick layer of fat poorly hidden behind a beard that had long ago turned prematurely white thanks to some poor genetics on his mother's side. When he saw Lionel, he placed the cigar on the window ledge and pushed himself from his comfortable leather chair. His thinking chair, he called it, though most of the courthouse staff referred to it as his drinking chair.

"Yes, television," the judge said. "It's the twenty-first century, and do you have any idea how many times a case of mine has gotten me on television?"

Lionel tilted his head to the side as he thought, then frowned. "I don't know."

"Not once. I've been a judge for twenty years, and I haven't been on television once. It's embarrassing. Henry Petty graduated eighteenth in my class, and his practice runs commercials nightly in Florida. I've seen them. He stands there in a cheap suit and a cheap rug and promises a fast settlement. Practically guarantees one. That brown-noser had no business graduating any higher than fortieth, and he's on TV seven nights a week. I ask you, is that justice?"

"No, it's not, Your Honor."

"You're damn right it's not. Jay Rodgers graduated thirty-forth, and he's a consultant for some news network," the judge said. He fortified himself with a deep sip from his glass. "He couldn't put Osama bin Laden away for life if you gave him a jury of New York City firemen and he's a television consultant. It's pathetic."

"It really is, sir."

"So what are we going to do about it?"

"Do? What can we do?"

The judge crossed his office, stepping around the pile of unsorted mail and his bag of golf clubs. He pulled up a chair at the table where Lionel worked, and he exhaled a scotch-laden breath from the effort.

"Where's the docket for this week?" he asked. "Maybe there's something in there we can use to get some publicity."

Lionel reached past the mail to the short stack of folders that comprised the fifth circuit's docket for the next week. It was immediately obvious the pickings would be slim, but Judge Huntz didn't comment until he was finished flipping through the folders and reading the cases within.

"You know, Lionel, I'm a humble man," he said. "You know that, don't you?"

"Of course, sir."

"I worked my way through college and law school. I was the first in my family to get educated, and never once did I feel like the world owed me a thing. I firmly believe a man needs to work for what he wants and be happy with what he gets. I believe that, Lionel. I'm happy. I love my job. I've got no reason to complain."

"None at all."

"That's right, none at all. But I do feel my life is missing something. Some small bit of affirmation that I don't get toiling anonymously in my courtroom." The judge drank again from his glass. Then he placed it on the table and slid it away, empty. "I've done some good work from this bench, but some days, I feel like a thoroughbred that's being used as a horsey ride. I could do so much more, Lionel. So much more if I just had a chance. If more people saw what I was doing, if they saw the kind of judge I am, I could do so much more.

"I'd be more helpful than Henry Petty and his bad hairpiece, that's for sure. I need a case big enough to get my name out there. Once my legal mind is a matter of public record, maybe I could take a step up to the federal level. Or maybe someone would let me write that book about my top ten cases I've wanted to write for so long." The judge fanned the docket folders on the table, then shuffled them back into a pile. "Or maybe I could even get a show of my own. The sky's the limit once you get on television, Lionel."

"I'm sure it is, Your Honor."

Judge Huntz stopped playing with the folders and locked eyes with his young clerk. "I need your help, Lionel."

"*My* help? What can I do?"

"You can help me find the case that gets me on television. Once we have that case, we're on our way."

"Our way?"

"A rising tide lifts all ships, Lionel. If you help me out here, I won't forget it."

"I appreciate that, Your Honor. I'm a little confused, though. How do I find a case for you? Don't we have to wait for someone to do something that rates a big court case?"

"Of course we do," the judge said. "But something must be going on out there that has a local angle we can exploit. Maybe some terrorist passed through town on his way to do his dirty work. Or maybe there's enough people in town to bring a class action suit."

"Against whom?"

"Against anyone. Big tobacco. A pharmaceutical company. A car manufacturer. I don't know, but there must be something out there. You know what the problem is?"

"What?"

"The problem is the lawyers around here aren't motivated. We've got no sharks in my jurisdiction. If we had some sharks around here, I wouldn't have to figure out how to find a big case. There'd be big cases breaking down the door. Oh, what I wouldn't give for some movie star to slap a local. Could you imagine my face on *Entertainment Tonight* every night the trial dragged on?"

"Not really, sir."

"Well, you'd better start imagining, Lionel. Think big. It's time for the two of us to shine."

Lionel put the mail aside and reached over for the docket files. Judge Huntz raised a hand in warning.

"After you finish with my mail, of course," he said.

"Of course, Your Honor."

As Lionel returned to the mail, Judge Huntz retrieved his glass and carried it to the small bar in the far corner of the room. He poured himself a fresh drink and pondered the conversation he'd just had. He was excited by the possibilities now that he'd brought Lionel on board.

Just two days later, Lionel Baker entered Judge Huntz's chambers and, at first, thought His Honor had slipped out the back door. The judge was known to sneak off for a drink at Lunny's Tavern down the block every now and then. Lionel was placing a slim stack of mail on the table when he saw the judge hunched over a book in the corner, seemingly oblivious to everything around him. He was either lost in thought or he'd fallen asleep. Lionel had seen both since taking this job.

"That you, Lionel?" the judge asked, ruling out the sleep theory. Lionel was a little disappointed about that. He'd hoped to slip in, drop off the mail, and slip out unnoticed. Judge Huntz had nothing on his docket today, and when he came to the courthouse on days with nothing on his docket, he got chatty. Lionel rarely got any work done on days like this.

"Yes, sir. Just dropping off the mail."

"Come here a second. I need you to look at something."

Lionel rolled his eyes as he approached. It was always a crapshoot when the judge wanted to show him something. The something could be anything from a disturbing piece of evidence to a picture of one of his grandkids, and whatever it was usually came with a long story attached. So much for leaving early today.

Judge Huntz was slumped in an easy chair with a large map unfolded on his lap. In one hand he held a newspaper, and in the other a thick paperbound volume of the many rules that made up the tri-county judicial system. Before now, Lionel wouldn't have thought the judge had more than a passing familiarity with the rule book. As Lionel got closer, he noticed the map had several lines drawn across it. A pencil and eraser rested on the judge's knee.

"Lionel, I've been checking the maps against the accident accounts in the paper, but I'm not sure I've done this right," Judge Huntz said. "Could you double-check for me?"

Lionel took the newspaper and book that were offered to him, then juggled them with the map the judge handed over.

"What am I looking for?" he asked.

"I'm trying to figure out if the accident happened in our jurisdiction." The accident. It was the story of the year, as far as the local media was concerned. On the surface, it was a simple car accident. Yesterday morning, an SUV had run over a drunk out on one of the back roads. But the driver was the owner of the region's largest chain of retail stores. And the victim was a stock boy in one of those stores. The media frenzy within the confines of the tri-county area was worse than anything Lionel had ever seen. He'd been wondering how long it would take for the story to hit the judge's radar.

"Oh, I see," he said. "I don't need a map to answer that one."

"Why not?"

"This accident is the talk of the town. Since yesterday morning, everyone's been looking into whose case it could be, if it turns into a case," Lionel said.

"Oh, it turns into a case all right. I can feel it. So who gets it?"

"The case, if there is one, falls into our jurisdiction," Lionel said.

"Hot dog. That's what I thought." The judge pulled back his map and observed the lines he'd drawn with a look of pride on his soft, puffy face. "This is gonna be big, Lionel. Huge."

"What is?"

"This case. This is the chance I was waiting for. Once I preside over this case, my mug gets on televisions across the country."

"I guess so," Lionel said. He wasn't feeling anywhere near the enthusiasm the judge was displaying.

"In fact, maybe we shouldn't wait until the case starts," Judge Huntz said. "We should probably be proactive on this one. First thing tomorrow, put in a call to the local affiliates. See if they could use another legal expert on this case."

"Not a good idea, Your Honor."

"Why not?" The judge's brows, thick gray caterpillars that threatened to meet in the middle of his forehead someday, furrowed and looked like they were spoiling for a fight. The judge's vaguely unkempt mustache also took on a grim cast whenever the judge's opinion was questioned. This same expression had intimidated some of the best lawyers in the tri-county area, but it didn't work on Lionel anymore. The judge didn't keep clerks more than a couple of years for this very reason. A clerk was no good to him if he didn't feel a little intimidated by Judge Huntz.

"Because if you go on the air as a legal expert, you've shown a bias, and you can't try the case," Lionel said.

"That's not true."

"I think it is. And even if it isn't, do you want whatever you say on TV to be used during the inevitable appeal?"

Judge Huntz frowned as he thought this over.

"But you know, since you don't even know if you'd get the case, or if it would go to one of the other three judges in the rotation, maybe you should take this chance to get on TV like you wanted to," Lionel added.

"I'll get the case, Lionel. Don't worry about that."

"How do you know?"

"I'm senior jurist around here. That fact allows me to supersede the rotation whenever I deem it necessary."

The judge was right about this. In the last couple of years, he'd taken to removing his name from the rotation whenever a particularly knotty case turned up on the docket. Some of the other clerks had taken to calling him "The Dodger" because of his unerring instincts when identifying difficult cases and then avoiding them. It would be entirely unprecedented for him to jump ahead and take a case he didn't have to, but these were special circumstances. Lionel briefly wondered if he could get some betting action on this one. He didn't think there would be anyone else in the courthouse willing to bet that the judge would take this case, based on the historical record.

"May I be honest with you, Your Honor?"

"You don't need to ask me that, Lionel. You should feel free to always be completely honest with me. Within reason, of course. What's on your mind?"

"It just sounds wrong, you wrangling to get this case so you can be on TV," Lionel said. He still had the county rulebook in his hand, and he stood it on end on his knees as a very sad-looking shield from the judge's potential wrath. "It's like you're trying to take advantage of this accident for your own personal gain. It doesn't look good."

The judge frowned again, then sighed, and his face took on an exasperated expression.

"Lionel, in the last day and a half you've seen nothing but people trying to take advantage of this case," he said. "You think that boy gets helped any by newspaper articles telling us he liked Yoo Hoo when he was a kid and in fourth grade he grew pumpkins for a science experiment? I read both of those stories this morning, by the way. Of course he doesn't, but if someone buys the paper to read about those things, someone's making money off of it.

"All I want is a chance to shine, Lionel. A chance to show people beyond this building that I'm a good judge and that I have a vision of justice that other people can and should emulate. The only way I could ever possibly earn anything from this is if someone offers me a chance to make a TV show. And to be honest, I don't even know if I'd take the show if it was offered. Too much work, and I don't think I have the energy to do it anyway." Judge Huntz pushed himself up from his slouch and settled back into the chair.

"I want this case, and I want people to be able to watch this case, but I can promise you that when the case is over, there won't be any reason for anyone to think anything unseemly about my work. My life has been the law for nearly twenty-seven years, and there's no chance I'd throw that away for a shot on CNN. Do you understand that?"

"Yes, Your Honor, I understand. I'm sorry I doubted you."

"Now for Fox News, maybe. But CNN? Hell no." The judge winked as he spoke, then began folding up his map. "If there's a case, I get the case. And there's gonna be a case, I can assure you of that. And that case will be handled with the utmost respect for both plaintiff and defendant."

"I understand that, Your Honor. Once again, I apologize." Lionel felt his face burning from embarrassment.

"No need to apologize, but you do need to skedaddle. I've got work to do."

Once Lionel was gone, the judge approached his desk and struggled to organize the piles of folders stacked high, a task that became more and more difficult every passing day. There were files here from old cases that needed attention, current cases he might have to preside over, and several appeals, which were always the worst. He dumped those off to the side for checking later, after everything else was done. Next to the appeals was a small pile of folders sent to him by his nephew from California. This was the pile of most importance to him.

He paused to skim the first page of the proposal on top of the pile. According to the proposal, the judge would preside over a legal reality show. Each week, Judge Huntz would sentence a wrongdoer to take the place of an injured party, and then the show's cameras would follow that person around as he or she attempted to hold someone else's life together for the duration of the sentence. The proposal said the judge would have ultimate authority of the length and severity of the sentences, but Judge Huntz couldn't see such a show lasting for more than a couple of weeks. Scratch that one.

He'd asked his nephew, a writer for some game show the judge never watched, to write him up a few solid proposals he could use on the day when his legal work propelled him to the appropriate level of fame. These folders were what he got back, and they'd sat unread for several months. Now that this car accident case was blooming, the judge decided it was time to see what options he had. He'd envisioned something along the lines of *The People's Court*. Maybe he could've even landed *The People's Court* itself. They'd let Ed Koch host it, so obviously their standards were low. But after flipping through several folders, he realized his nephew had not sent him the next *The People's Court*.

He pulled another folder from the proposal pile. In this one, he'd preside over a household of people guilty of small-claims-level crimes, and each week he was to rule on which houseguest got evicted from the house. After the mock trial, he was supposed to tell the evictee, "I sentence you to eviction."

The judge was about to toss this folder aside, too, when an idea struck him. He picked up a pen and crossed out that line, then replaced it with "Justice is served." He closed the folder and used it to start a "maybe" pile.

Just how many of his classmates had their own reality show? Exactly none. Judge Huntz leaned back and imagined the premiere.

"*Justice Is Served*, starring Judge Andrew Huntz," he said. The judge smiled. That would be some good television right there.

# Lord Coke Unbenched

"By no possibility, a lesser sum can be satisfaction to the plaintiff for a greater sum; but the gift of a horse, a hawk or robe, etc. in satisfaction is good."

—Lord Coke, *Pinnel's Case*

We imagine him, Lord Coke,
With horse and hawk and robe,
Slanting down some windy slope:

All law forgotten; only the fall
Of earth below him; the call
Of the spring hawk; the small

Sound of prey a-scutter
In the autumn field.
                    And we mutter,
"This is the far other

Side of law: all binding rules
Relinquished in the light of cool
October sun; the pool

Of brainy wisdom drained
From the doing flesh."
Loose-reined,
The horse makes a sane

Clatter of hooves a-canter; we grope
Through books, which, opened,
Fill quiet rooms with wordy smoke.

Still, with fierce satisfaction, Lord Coke,
Bearing hawk and wearing robe,
Calls wildly on the windy slope.

—*Dan Gunter*

# CONTRIBUTORS

**Michael Del Muro** currently works as a freshman English teacher at a private high school east of Los Angeles. He previously worked as a newspaper reporter at a local Los Angeles County newspaper. He also holds a master's degree from the University of Southern California in professional writing.

**Jeffrey A. Dickerson** has been a litigator in Reno, Nevada, since 1987. He is fifty-two years old, has been married for twenty-seven years, and has two grown children. His passions are fighting for civil rights during the week and playing with his pugs on the weekends.

Former process server, English teacher, radio station copywriter, and advertising agency creative director, **Jack Ewing** has written over one hundred million words for print, radio, television, Internet, and other media since 1960. He has lived in Idaho since 1980.

**Joseph A. Farina** has been a barrister and solicitor in Sarnia, Ontario, Canada, for thirty-five years. He has been published in many poetry journals in Canada, the United States, and Europe. He is the author of two books of poetry, *The Cancer Chronicles* and *Ghosts of Water Street*.

**Tom Green** works too hard and writes when he can. Occasionally, he can be found updating www.themostcommonsideeffectisnausea.com, his blog, or www.treetoplounge.com, his website devoted to humor and fiction. He does most of his writing while riding the bus to work.

**Dan Gunter** is a husband, father, and attorney practicing law at a midsize Seattle firm. Before attending law school, he taught writing at the college level and edited scholarly books. His poetry has been published in *Lucid Rhythms, 14 x 14,* and *Quill & Parchment*.

Coming from a family of attorneys and the occasional judge, **Juliet Hubbell**, to everyone's confusion, chose instead to write. She makes a living outside the courtroom and inside the lecture hall, teaching writing to college students at Arapahoe Community College.

**Liz Hufford** is the published author of poems, short stories, articles, and essays. She has a Masters of Arts degree and a well-used passport. Hiking the Inca Trail to Machu Picchu and snorkeling off Bora Bora are some of her travel highlights. She once lived south of Utopia and north of Paradise, but now resides on Shangri La in a desert garden that might make Eve envious.

**John Lambremont, Sr.** is a Pushcart Prize-nominated poet from Baton Rouge, Louisiana. He has a B.A. in Creative Writing and a J.D. from L.S.U. During the last two years, John's poems have been published or accepted internationally by over thirty reviews and journals, including *Chaffey Review*, *Sugar House Review*, *Red River Review*, *A Hudson View*, *Taj Mahal Review*, and *Lilliput Review*. His full-length volume of retrospective poems, *Whiskey, Whimsy, & Rhymes* (2009), is available at amazon.com and all major bookstore websites.

**Anthony J. Mohr**'s short stories and essays have appeared in, among other places, *Bibliophilos*, *The Christian Science Monitor*, the *Chicken Soup for the Soul* series, *Freckles To Wrinkles*, *The LBJ: Avian Life - Literary Arts*, *Oracle*, *Word Riot*, and *ZYZZYVA*. Three of his pieces have been nominated for the Pushcart Prize. By day, he is a judge on the Superior Court of California, County of Los Angeles, where he has presided over misdemeanor and felony trials and, currently, civil cases in the court's complex litigation program.

**Leslie B. Neustadt** is a graduate of the University of Rochester and Temple Law School and practiced law for almost thirty years. She was an assistant attorney general in the Appeals and Opinions Bureau and the Consumer Frauds and Protection Bureau of the New York State Attorney General's Office for seventeen years before retiring. Her work has been published in, among others, *Awareness Magazine*, *Cure Magazine*, *Akros Review*, *Mused: BellaOnline Literary Review*, and *Poetica*. She is a member of the International Women's Writers Guild and the Hudson Valley Writers Guild and lives in Niskayuna, New York.

**Randall Patterson** has lived in Houston since birth, where he has worked as an insurance adjuster, attorney, and high school English teacher. He is the author of many novels, stories, poems, and screenplays, including *The Book of the Lam*, which concerns the downward spiral of a lawyer on the run, and is available from the usual online sources.

**Tony Press** lives near the Pacific Ocean. He practiced law for a bunch of years before stopping in time. His writings appear in, among others, *Rio Grande Review, SFWP Journal, Boston Literary Magazine, Menda City Review, Foundling Review, Temenos, MacGuffin, Shine Journal, Lichen,* Toasted Cheese, Quay, 5x5, Contemporary Verse 2, and the anthology *Crab Lines off the Pier*.

**Charles Reynard** serves as circuit judge in central Illinois. His poems have appeared on WGLT's Poetry Radio, in the anthology *Where We Live Illinois Poets*, the 2004 *Emily Dickinson Awards* anthology, and the literary journals *AfterHours, Apocalypse, Crab Orchard Review,* and *National Catholic Reporter*. He is co-editor (with Judith Valente) of *Twenty Poems to Nourish Your Soul* (2006, Loyola Press). He is the author of the chapbook *The Utility of Heart Break* (The Pikestaff Press, 2010).

**Kristin Roedell** is a Northwest poet and retired attorney. Her poems have appeared in many mediums, including print, online, and radio. Selected poetry appears in *Switched on Gutenberg, Flutter, damselfly press,* and Eclectica; other poems are forthcoming from *Chest, Seeding the Snow,* Ginosko, and Frostwriting.

A 2011 Pushcart Prize nominee, **Cynthia Schwartzberg Edlow**'s debut poetry collection, *The Day Judge Spencer Learned the Power of Metaphor,* is forthcoming from Salmon Poetry in 2011. She has new poems appearing in *James Dickey Review* and the international anthology *Dogs Singing (A Tribute Anthology)*.